SHAKESPEARE
AND THE NATURAL CONDITION

SHAKESPEARE

AND THE NATURAL CONDITION

Geoffrey Bush

Harvard University Press, Cambridge, 1956

TO MY TWO EARLIEST READERS

This essay, in more or less its present form, was delivered as a series of lectures under the auspices of the Lowell Institute at the Old South Meeting House in Boston during the month of January, 1955. Mr. Robert Fitzgerald's translation of Oedipus at Colonus *is quoted by permission of Harcourt, Brace and Company, Inc. I should like to express my indebtedness and gratitude to the Society of Fellows of Harvard University; to Miss Ethel Seaton; to two of the many critics of Shakespeare, Mr. D. G. James and Mr. Arthur Sewell; and in particular to Mr. Alfred Harbage and Mr. Harry Levin, critics of both Shakespeare and this essay. Such an acknowledgement does not cover my obligations to Mr. Levin.*

SHAKESPEARE
AND THE NATURAL CONDITION

I

THE ORDER AND CONTINUANCE OF NATURE

When Sir Andrew Aguecheek and Sir Toby Belch are in admirable fooling, Sir Andrew announces proudly: "Ay, he does well enough if he be dispos'd, and so do I too. He does it with a better grace, but I do it more natural." Not all of us would say with such enthusiasm that we were natural fools. But each of us belongs to nature; a part of ourselves is natural, and we are a part of the natural world.

I should like to consider what it means to Shakespeare's characters to belong to nature. Recent criticism has suggested that Shakespeare's characters, and what they do and believe, should be seen in relation to the Elizabethan idea of natural order. I would, to some small extent, take issue with this recent criticism. But others have spoken of these matters with a better grace, and I should say at once that I have no absolute conclusions to reach; there are no conclusions to be had about nature, or about Shakespeare's plays. His business is with the imagination; perhaps the most important thing we can say about his plays is that they come to no conclusions; and concerning nature John Donne wrote with some impatience: "This terme the law of Nature, is so variously and unconstantly deliver'd, as I confesse I read it a hundred times before I understand it once."

The term "nature" is variously delivered in Shakespeare's plays. But there are two ways in which nature has always been understood: it means both the nature of things, and natural things in themselves. It is a name for both the law of the world, and the world itself. These are the two ways in which nature is defined in *The French Academy*: "When they speake generallie of nature, they make two principall kindes: the one spirituall, intelligible and the unchangeable beginning of motion and rest, or rather the vertue, efficient, and preserving cause of all things: the other, sensible, mutable, and subject to generation and corruption, respecting all things that have life, and shall have end."

To speak more briefly, *The French Academy* goes on, "Nature is the order and continuance of the works of God." But it is an order and continuance that has two aspects: it is an idea of natural law, and the fact of natural things. Nature means both the unchanging natural principle of the world, the preserving cause of all things, and the changing face of the world, all things that have life and shall have end. It is a name for whatever is natural, *natura naturata*, and for the reason why it is natural, *natura naturans*. In the last book of *The Faerie Queene* the Sergeant Order is a servant of the Goddess Nature; but nature is also represented as a changing pageant of the seasons and months and hours. And the Goddess Nature herself is a figure of double beauty, old and young, changing and unchanging, seen and unseen.

Nature is a fact of change and an idea beyond change; its double aspect is what places human nature in so dramatic a position, created sick, as Fulke Greville wrote, but commanded to be sound; and through this double aspect Shakespeare's characters, at their greatest moments, become involved both with things in themselves and with the meaning of things. When Hamlet waits for the fencing match, he says: "Sir, I will walk here in the hall." It is the breathing time of day with him; there is misgiving in his heart, but he says to Horatio: "If it be now, 'tis not to come; if it be not to come, it will be now; if it be not now, yet it will come: the readiness is all." We know nothing more about Hamlet than we did before; he has promised to do no more than walk in the hall; yet he seems to have come to terms with his world. It is the most mysterious moment in the play, a point of unexpected stillness and security and at the same time of strange unease, when every possibility of his natural situation is brought into our minds. There is a similar moment in *King Lear*. After the storm, when Lear wakes in the arms of Cordelia, he tells her: "You are a spirit, I know." Lear is mistaken; she is not a spirit; yet she seems so. These are points in experience when natural life seems to belong both to time and to what is beyond time; when Hamlet is acting and not acting, and Cordelia is a spirit and not a spirit; when we are made most aware of what it means to act and believe within both the aspects of natural life; and these moments are what I should like to speak of.

II

But what are we able to say of these moments? Nothing is concluded; they are events in which character is implicated in both aspects of nature at once.

It has been proposed by recent criticism that Shakespeare's vision looks toward the further aspect of nature: that it was shaped by the Elizabethan idea of natural order, the doctrine of the first chapter of *The Governor* or the first book of the *Ecclesiastical Polity*, a picture of a world of arrangement and harmony. "A doctrine of Nature," Mr. E. C. Knowlton says, "constitutes the core of the view of life held by Shakespeare," and according to this doctrine the "purposes of conduct and of art are to know Nature and to follow her." But *Hamlet* and *King Lear* are pictures of natural disorder; there is great

5

pain attending what Hamlet and Lear come to know about nature, and there is great doubt whether they should follow nature. There is doubt, I think, whether a doctrine of natural order constitutes the core of Shakespeare's view of life. Certainly the doctrine of order is everywhere in Elizabethan writing and in Shakespeare's plays; it can be said to shape the vision of the histories and comedies, and the most famous of all its Elizabethan expressions is Ulysses' speech in *Troilus and Cressida*. Yet everywhere in Shakespeare's plays there is profound concern for the other aspect of natural life, natural things in themselves. The doctrine of order does not explain all that Shakespeare saw in *Hamlet* and *King Lear;* it is too large a philosophy, or not large enough, to explain how his vision links both aspects of the natural situation, the continuance of things and things in themselves.

There is a tendency of the mind to seek out meaning; the Elizabethan doctrine of order belongs to this effort toward conclusive statement. The doctrine of order has not survived: we no longer believe in degree and hierarchy, or in the Goddess Nature; the wench is dead, and her natural law has fallen in station, through the centuries, from the decree of God in the Renaissance, to the voice of reason in the eighteenth century, to the cry of the Romantic imagination, and now to mutterings from the unconscious. The history of the great chain of being, Mr. Arthur O. Lovejoy says, "is the history of a failure; more precisely and more justly, it is the record of an experiment in thought carried on for many centuries by many great and lesser minds, which can now be seen to have had an instructive negative outcome." And while the idea of order has not survived, *Hamlet* and *King Lear* have survived: they belong to a different enterprise of the mind, concerned with matters more personal, more obscure, and more exacting of our fears and affections. They are an experiment in thought that did not end in failure; and what is striking about them is that their outcome is so incomplete and inconclusive.

Shakespeare's art is traditionally associated with nature. But the purpose of this traditional association has been to show Shakespeare's adherence to persons and events in themselves. His first editors, Heminge and Condell, said that Shakespeare was "a happie imitator of Nature." What they meant was that he wrote with a natural ease: "His mind and hand went together: And what he thought, he uttered with that easinesse, that wee have scarce received from him a blot in his papers." Perhaps there was scarcely a blot in his papers; other writers have said that their best work was written easily; and it was a remark of this sort that caused Ben Jonson to deliver his brief and notable response: "My answer hath beene, would he had blotted a thousand." [Whether he did so or not, there is a quality of naturalness about Shakespeare's characters and situations, and about the art itself.] A later editor, Dr. Johnson, said that Shakespeare was "above all writers, at least above all modern writers, the poet of nature." Dr. Johnson meant that [Shakespeare's plays are pictures of the variety of natural fact: they are works "exhibiting the real state of sublunary nature, which partakes of good and evil, joy and sorrow, mingled with endless variety of proportion and innumerable modes of combination; and expressing the course of the world, in which the loss of one is the gain of another; in which, at the same time, the reveller is hasting to his wine, and the mourner burying his friend; in which the malignity of one is sometimes defeated by the frolick of another; and many mischiefs and many benefits are done and hindered without design."] In this manner Shakespeare is a poet of nature indeed; for variety, as Sir Walter Raleigh wrote in the Preface to *The History of the World,* is a primary attribute of nature: "there being nothing wherein Nature so much triumpheth, as in dissimilitude. From whence it commeth, that there is found so great diversity of opinions; so strong a contrariety of inclinations; so many naturall and unnaturall; wise, foolish; manly, and childish affections, and passions in Mortall Men." [These qualities in Shakespeare's work of naturalness and ease, and of engagement to the variety of persons and things, are what prevent conclusions, and make the vision itself, through the diversity of its opinions, seem without design.]

There is another traditional judgment, besides the judgment that Shakespeare was a poet of nature; it is that he was a poet without art. When Ben Jonson wrote his memorial poem to Shakespeare, he said first, as so many others were to say later, that the Goddess Nature herself was proud of Shakespeare's designs. But in an earlier and less guarded moment Jonson said shortly that "Shakspear wanted Arte." And in our own time another severe and learned classical poet has remarked briefly that *Hamlet* is "most certainly an artistic failure." Dr. Johnson thought that Shakespeare wrote with the power of nature, but he confessed that Shakespeare seemed also to write without any moral purpose. Shakespeare does not supply us, Edward Dowden said, with a doctrine, with an interpretation, with a revelation. And most recently Mr. D. G. James thinks that Shakespeare wrote "without a philosophy," and that in *King Lear* he looked upon the world with a "bleak and merely exploratory vision." Certainly there is justice in this traditional opinion. What Dr. Johnson said of poetry in general is true especially of Shakespeare's plays — they belong to those human works of which the excellence is not absolute and definite, but gradual and comparative. There are no characters in the plays who tell us all that Shakespeare means; his imagination is both within them and without, proposing possibilities, hints and guesses, and statements that are, as it were, unfinished.

Milton wrote in *Areopagitica* that Truth came once into

the world in a perfect shape, most glorious to look on, and now she is scattered in a thousand pieces. Truth displays one colored ensign, Chapman said, while the world pursues ten thousand colors. But the ten thousand colors of the world are what Shakespeare's vision makes known; his concern is with the scattered fragments of truth that reside in the actions and beliefs of particular men and women. He keeps at all times, as Coleridge said, on the high road of life, and in the main march of human affections. Mr. Alfred Harbage adds that Shakespearian tragedy is a high road leading home, telling us what we have always known. Surely this is true. But which of us knows his home? The tragic journey toward what we have always known is never completed; what is important about it is the journeying; poetry, in Mr. Archibald MacLeish's phrase, is a "continuing action," an involvement in knowing that is never ended.

The attachment to particular persons and events characterizes most of English poetry; the Western tradition in art is an endorsement of the importance of individual natural fact. Perhaps this is a result of Christianity and the other movements toward individualism in modern Western thought; whatever the reason, there is a difference between the architectural clarity of Greek tragedy and the engagement to things in themselves that is represented in the writing of even the most philosophic of Renaissance poets, Chapman or Milton. *Paradise Lost* has an epic design, but the subject is the event through which humanity forfeited a share in its own grand design; and the moment toward which Milton's vision is moving comes when Adam and Eve, hand in hand, through Eden take their solitary way. This commitment of English literature to things in themselves issues most fully in Shakespeare's plays; and through this commitment *Hamlet* and *King Lear* are a way of knowing that is itself "natural." His art, like nature, has a double aspect, an attachment to persons and

9

events that in its final moments suggests a continuance of meaning.

III

⌊ We think of Shakespeare's plays as a kind of knowledge. Hamlet tells the Players that the purpose of playing is to hold the mirror up to nature; a play makes nature known to itself. And near the end of Lear's storm, after we have been an audience to the worst of Lear's suffering, Edgar says:

> When we our betters see bearing our woes,
> We scarcely think our miseries our foes.
> Who alone suffers suffers most i' th' mind,
> Leaving free things and happy shows behind;
> But then the mind much sufferance doth o'erskip
> When grief hath mates, and bearing fellowship.

There is comfort in watching the suffering of others; it is a means of knowing our own griefs, and of finding them, perhaps, in everyone. We reach a sense of community, and by the "art of known and feeling sorrows" we discover ourselves. Certainly at the end of *Hamlet* and *King Lear* there is a sense of comfort, and of knowledge; something of great importance has been discovered about natural life. But what has been concluded, and what agreement has been reached? Nothing is said in *Hamlet* and *King Lear* that has the certainty of the knowledge offered by Shakespeare's two most distinguished contemporaries in the theater. Chapman and Webster take sides, and we know where they stand; their plays are comprehensive statements about the natural condition.⌉

In Chapman's vision things and the continuance of things are closely allied. A man is built with God's finger; the world is constructed perfect and free; and a man's chief virtue is glad obedience to the high and general cause. The world and the law of the world are a single reality; time and its continuance are joined in ourselves through right action and right reason. It is Webster's judgment, on the other hand, that the persons and events of natural life are far removed from the arrangement that gives them meaning: heaven fashioned us of nothing, and we bring ourselves to nothing; the soul in the body is a lark in a cage, looking toward a distant heaven; our natural life is a long war, a general mist of error, a slow misery that ends in the moment of fright and dazzle when we may win a kind of virtue by the manner in which we encounter death. The world and its reason are divorced, and to do and believe rightly is to flee the world and hope for grace. The positions taken by Chapman and Webster are as contrary as they could well be; they belong, more or less, to the philosphic traditions that are associated with the names of Aquinas and Augustine, and in the Renaissance with Hooker and Calvin. They are traditions that are a part of our most fundamental ways of thinking; to put the matter most simply, they are estimates of how near or how far things are from the significance of things. Things and their signif- icance are in close conjunction in Aquinas and Hooker, and in Chapman's plays. In Augustine and Calvin things are di- vided from their significance, and judgments of this sort inform the metaphysical shudder of Webster's tragedies; through the consequence of our ancient calamity in Eden there is no good in us, and what restoration is possible is the work of intervening grace.

The plays of Chapman and Webster are *drames à thèse*. Chapman's plays are constructed to demonstrate a philosophy, and Webster's to exhibit human beings in every posture of unhappiness. "I would have these things," one of Chapman's characters says, "Brought upon stages." In the direct state- ments that Chapman and Webster propose, and through the open assault that their plays make upon our minds, the world and the stage become one: "I account this world," the Duch- ess of Malfi says, "a tedious Theatre," and another of Webster's characters kills someone in a mist — such a mistake, he says, as he has often seen in a "play." There is the same equation between life and the theater in what Hamlet tells the Players; it gives to Shakespeare's poetic and dramatic vision much of its moral weight; but it is an equation that in *Hamlet* and *King Lear* leads to a different kind of statement, and another way of knowing.

IV

Two other contemporaries of Shakespeare's undertook to propose conclusive explanations of nature. Some parts of Spenser's *Faerie Queene* and Bacon's *Instauratio Magna* were written within a dozen years of each other, and within the same short period Shakespeare was carrying out his poetic and dramatic exploration of nature. This in itself, as Mr. James says of Shakespeare's work and Bacon's, is a thought to give us pause: that at the same moment in history these three great endeavors were launched, a religious explanation of nature, a scientific explanation, and a poetic and dramatic experiment that is committed wholly to neither things nor meaning.

Spenser's religious vision in *The Faerie Queene* turns toward the meaning of things. His Goddess Nature is a twofold figure, including in herself both the world and the design of the world; the natural changes of the world are a part of her pattern. And it is toward a still greater pattern that Spenser looks in the last lines of Book VII; though the Goddess Nature can explain mutability, Spenser looks beyond her explanation to the time "when no more *Change* shall be." *The Faerie Queene* directs us beyond the natural world to a religious order; the events, Spenser wrote in his letter to Sir Walter Raleigh, are "a continued Allegory, or darke conceit," standing for greater events in a further order and continuance. But it was Bacon's plan to isolate and explore natural events by themselves: to perfect (in the English of James Spedding) "a natural philosophy pure and unmixed." The *Novum Organum,* he said, was his part "towards the commencement of the great undertaking," the enterprise in which he was building in the human understanding "a true model of the world, such as it is in fact, not such as a man's own reason would have it to be." It cannot be said that Bacon's vision excludes the religious explanation of nature, or that Spenser's excludes the secular explanation; but Spenser's tendency is to join these explanations and Bacon's is to set them apart. What is in question is whether the temporal aspect of the world is an arrangement that would explain itself, if it were fully understood, or whether, because it is part of a divine arrangement, it leans on a further explanation, already partly revealed. From the history of later thought we know that Bacon prevailed. There exists now the division between religion and science that Bacon instituted when he distinguished between their two manners of understanding: "The knowledge of man is as the waters, some descending from above, and some springing from beneath; the one informed by the light of nature, the other inspired by divine revelation."

The Faerie Queene and the *Novum Organum* were not written in debate; Bacon was not the first natural philosopher, nor the first to distinguish between the ways of apprehending the two aspects of nature; and Spenser set down what he considered to be the common knowledge of all men. But their visions represent, at a time of philosophic change, the way that thought had taken and the way that thought was to take; they represent the explanations of nature that were made in the centuries before 1600 and that have been made since.

We are able to consider Shakespeare's plays at these crossroads of thought, when two great movements of the human spirit, endorsements of the unity or the division of experience, began to go their separate ways. We can, to some degree, place Chapman and Webster on these different roads. It is clear enough that Spenser and Chapman belong together in their classical and Christian humanism; they would see things and the continuance of things as a single whole. It is less clear, but I think it can be argued, that Bacon and Webster are to be associated in their division of things and meaning. They each put their trust in a different aspect of nature — Bacon looks toward the world and Webster toward what is beyond the world — but either choice belongs to the trend of thought that has resulted in the modern view of experience as divided and fragmentary. Bacon and Webster are committed to their different conclusions, and Spenser and Chapman to another certainty; it is Shakespeare's natural and easy art that seems, in modern terms, to be "unengaged."

v

Bacon called his undertaking an "argument of hope." Both *The Faerie Queene* and the *Instauratio Magna* are arguments of hope, and efforts of the mind toward conclusions. Bacon and Spenser were aware of the incompleteness of all human knowledge, and of the cause, the far-off divine event at the beginning of the Christian history of nature; but their inquiry, as Bacon said, was "whether that commerce between the mind of man and the nature of things, which is more precious than anything on earth, or at least than anything that is of the earth, might by any means be restored to its perfect and original condition." There are loose ends in *The Faerie Queene,* and ends that will not fit, but in it Spenser included all the religious and ethical affairs of human life; Prince Arthur, Spenser wrote in his letter to Raleigh, is "the image of a brave knight, perfected in the twelve private morall vertues." Prince Arthur is a perfect image; and three years after Spenser wrote to Raleigh, Bacon wrote a letter to Sir William Cecil to explain his "vast contemplative ends" and to say that "I have taken all knowledge to be my province."

"I propose to establish," Bacon declared, "progressive stages of certainty." We know that his enterprise, though it prevailed, was not to be so successful as he dreamed. But his words are like a trumpet call; and there is a different sound to the soldiers' music that proclaims the death of Hamlet, or in Edgar's frail and hopeless flourish at the end of *King Lear*. While *The Faerie Queene* and the *Instauratio Magna* were never finished, and are only pieces of their authors' intentions, *Hamlet* and *King Lear* are in a more essential manner unfinished. When Una sees the Dwarf carrying the armor of the Red Cross Knight, she asks to hear "the wofull Tragedie." It is not a tragedy at all; the Red Cross Knight is not dead, he will conquer and marry, and his woes are comprehended in the great progression toward salvation. The story of Leyr and Cordelia is told in Book II of *The Faerie Queene,* and neither is this a tragic story; it is part of English history, and a step in the historical progress toward Elizabeth and Gloriana.

Bacon said that there are two kinds of contemplation: "the one, arduous and difficult in the beginning, leads out at last into the open country; while the other, seeming at first sight easy and free from obstruction, leads to pathless and precipitous places." *The Faerie Queene* and Bacon's natural philosophy would lead us to this open country; they would bring us, in Bacon's words, to stand upon the hill of Truth, where the air is always clear and serene. Spenser's Red Cross Knight stands on the hill of Contemplation and looks toward the New Jerusalem; and Bacon was called a Moses who led his people to the verge of the Promised Land. It is "heaven upon earth," Bacon said, "to have a man's mind move in

charity, rest in providence, and turn upon the poles of truth."
So both Bacon and Spenser would say, looking toward heaven
upon earth, or toward heaven itself.

From the hill of Truth, Bacon said, we see the errors and
wanderings and mists in the vale below. Yet these are the subject of Shakespeare's plays, the errors and wanderings, and the
moving accidents by flood and field; and his vision, while it
seems at first sight easy and natural, and expressed in the
beauty and formality of poetry, leads us at the end to pathless
and precipitous places, and extremities of the human spirit.
In *The Advancement of Learning,* Bacon gave his famous
judgment of poetry: it is a branch of human knowledge, and
one of the principal portions of learning, but "it doth raise
and erect the mind, by submitting the shews of things to the
desires of the mind; whereas reason doth buckle and bow the
mind unto the nature of things." The kind of poetry that
Bacon allowed to be nearest the truth was allegory, the poetry
of *The Faerie Queene,* where things in themselves are an emblem of the nature of things. There is no such correspondence
in *Hamlet* and *King Lear;* our pity and terror are for the
events as they are. *Hamlet* and *King Lear* are not statements
about action and belief; they are acting, and make-believe,
and the vision, in Bacon's words, is "a dream of learning." In
Hamlet the perfect image of the courtier, scholar, soldier is
quite, quite down; his life is a story of intendments gone
awry, of accidental judgments and purposes mistook. At the
end he seems to have reached an agreement with his situation:
but what has he done? His agreement is no more than to accept the challenge to the fencing match, and then it is neither
yes nor no, but only, "Sir, I will walk here in the hall." We
know only what Hamlet says about himself, and what he says
is unfinished; he breaks off, he has no more time to speak, and
"the rest is silence." And at the end of *King Lear* there is no
image of order; the figures on the stage form a picture of dis-

tress, and we that are young shall never live so long nor see so much. It is when Lear enters with Cordelia dead in his arms that Kent asks: "Is this the promis'd end?" And Edgar asks in return: "Or image of that horror?" Shakespeare's vision does not end with a revelation or a philosophy, or with progressive stages of certainty.

VI

But it was Shakespeare's first editors who said that "these Playes have had their triall alreadie, and stood out all Appeales." *Hamlet* and *King Lear,* no doubt, are Shakespeare's greatest plays; they are, at any rate, the plays in which nature is mentioned most often. They are the very seamark of an utmost sail; in *Hamlet* and *King Lear* Shakespeare explores the furthest reaches of what it means to belong both to things and to the continuance of things. And what I have to say about nature in *Hamlet* and *King Lear* is the consequence of a question asked by Mr. Arthur Sewell in his book *Character and Society in Shakespeare.* It is the question, Mr. Sewell says, around which Shakespeare fashioned his picture of the natural situation: "How shall man find the intersection between that which is in time and that which is out of time?" Or more simply: "What shall we do to be saved?"

Shakespeare's characters belong to time and the world; they have a natural constitution, natural passions, natural feeling, and natural reason. They are moved by excitements of their reason and their blood to share in the duties and pains and affections of natural life. In what they do and believe there is represented a deep involvement in persons and things; through this involvement Shakespeare's characters experience their profits and losses, and we are moved to pity and admiration by our understanding of the glories and mistakes of this involvement. Yet Shakespeare's characters are not wholly a part of the natural world. They are divided from their world;

they are made to stand at one remove from their situation, and to undertake the effort of knowing and replying to the world. Their world, as it were, takes on an identity of its own; it has a shape and voice, and addresses those within it. The moral laws of nature and of nations, Hector says, "speak aloud." The Ghost speaks aloud to Hamlet, and in the storm Lear is addressed by the elements. And at their greatest moments Shakespeare's characters make their reply; at the end of the tragic progress it belongs not only to their suffering, but to their honor, that they stand apart from the world. They know the world and judge it, and they step forward to make their own address; they strike an attitude in the face of the world, and announce that they are natural fools, that "I am Bottom the weaver," or that "This is I, Hamlet the Dane."

It is at these moments that their involvement in nature becomes most complicated and precious. For to belong to nature is to be involved in an arrangement that at its most distant points touches what is beyond things in themselves. There is "terror for that which is out of time," Mr. Sewell says, "and pity for that which is in time, and they make a single experience." This single experience is the end of Shakespeare's vision; it is, as it were, the Shakespearian moment. When Lear and Cordelia in prison will be God's spies, or when Hamlet tells Horatio that there is a special providence in the fall of a sparrow, moments seem to have been reached, at some remote limit of natural life, when there is made known the possibility of a settlement between the two aspects of nature.

It is not good, Bacon said, to remain too long in the theater; and having given his judgment of poetry Bacon turned to graver matters and would not stay for an answer. But Shakespeare's vision expresses itself through the words and gestures of the theater; it reaches toward a different advancement of our learning, a way of knowing and settling with the world by which we are drawn into the continuing action of poetry and the theater. What saddens us at Hamlet's death is that he has no more time to speak, and no further words with which to record his life; but it is a great comfort, and an argument of hope, that Horatio will report Hamlet and his cause aright. He will tell Hamlet's "story" in "this harsh world." [In the equation between the world and the theater, it is Shakespeare's perception that life itself is a dramatic situation of address and reply, expressed most easily and naturally in the small globe of the stage. There is a profound commerce between our lives and the gestures of the theater; it is Hamlet's most glorious accomplishment to have made his life into a "story." Shakespeare's vision reaches toward a settlement with nature that in the deepest sense is a poetic and dramatic settlement: not a moment of certainty, the point in T. S. Eliot's *Four Quartets* when through the relinquishment of things in themselves we arrive at the still center of the turning world; but a moment when natural life is addressed by every voice, by things and by the meaning of things; when the possibilities of natural life go beyond even the power of words, and when it is right and proper that the rest is silence, and that Hamlet should say:]

> O, I could tell you—
> But let it be.

II

COMEDY AND THE PERFECT IMAGE

The resolution of the temporal and the eternal occupies our minds in the progress of tragedy. There is a similar progress in comedy, a movement from things in themselves toward a moment of natural perfection; the end of comedy is the triumph of the idea of order. It is in the histories and comedies that Shakespeare's vision moves toward absolute conclusions: the histories and comedies are indeed arguments of hope, looking toward a promised end. Their motto is *respice finem*; in the broadest sense their endeavor belongs to Bacon's and Spenser's effort to reach certainty.

The immediate concern of the comedies is with persons and events; but above things in themselves, and governing what happens, is the idea of an ordered society. The idea shapes the plays, directing events toward a happy ending, and no natural fact can prevent it. The end of each comedy is the moment when society reaches a perfect idea of itself, and the progress of individual characters is toward this perfect idea: when they confront nature, their encounter is with a continuance that is guiding them toward the realization of themselves. Only the fools, Sir Andrew Aguecheek and Sir Toby Belch, stand aloof from the natural continuance; lovers join themselves to a persuasion that is leading society toward a dream of perfection. The comedies share the desire for complete statement; their vision is of character and event striving toward meaning; and to make possible the realization of meaning and order the art of comedy imposes meaning and directs what takes place. It is Shakespeare's art that to our delight arranges the happy endings; and this sense of the power and joy of art is at length represented in the figure of Prospero.

There are disguises and villains and storms off the seacoast of Bohemia, but the end of every comedy is marriage, in which the dream of order is triumphantly attained. "Marriage," George Eliot wrote in *Middlemarch*, "which has been the bourne of so many narratives, is still a great beginning, as it was to Adam and Eve." For the world, as Benedick admits, must be peopled; and as Parolles says bitterly, "Who cannot be crush'd with a plot?" The plot of comedy is matrimony, which carries all in its path; and in the formality and ceremony of a wedding the order of society is made perfect. A disobedient wife is "a foul contending rebel," but the rebels of the comedies are put down with a dispatch not achieved by the kings of the history plays. To the husband belongs what the Wife of Bath called sovereignty:

> Such duty as the subject owes the prince,
> Even such a woman oweth to her husband.

The rules of nature, Luciana tells her sister in *The Comedy of Errors,* teach the act of order to a household:

> Why, headstrong liberty is lash'd with woe.
> There's nothing situate under heaven's eye
> But hath his bound in earth, in sea, in sky.
> The beasts, the fishes, and the winged fowls
> Are their males' subjects and at their controls.
> Men, more divine, the masters of all these,
> Lords of the wide world and wild wat'ry seas,
> Indu'd with intellectual sense and souls,
> Of more preëminence than fish and fowls,

> Are masters to their females, and their lords.
> Then let your will attend on their accords.

Luciana speaks in couplets; for these are formal words, like Ulysses' speech in *Troilus and Cressida,* and a lesson in domestic degree. It is twenty lines later that Luciana speaks to her sister more womanly: "Here comes your man."

The natural continuance addresses the characters of the comedies with the lesson of love, but not too much love: its address is not what Acrasia represents in Book II of *The Faerie Queene,* a disordered incontinence. In *Venus and Adonis,* Venus pleads: "By law of nature thou art bound to breed." She is wrong; headstrong liberty is lashed with woe; and Adonis' reply puts love and desire in their true places in the natural order of sunshine and storm:

> Love comforteth like sunshine after rain,
> But Lust's effect is tempest after sun.

There is a deadly sexual affinity between the two hunters, Venus and the boar; they would both, Venus thinks, kill Adonis with their kissing. The theme of *Venus and Adonis,* and of its darker counterpart *Lucrece,* is the phrase from one of the sonnets, "Desire is death." Adonis and Lucrece are the victims of desire, and Venus is another victim; there is an affinity not only between Venus and the boar, but between Venus and poor Wat. Bushes catch at her legs, as briers scratch Wat's, and in her frenzy, as Wat cranks and crosses with a thousand doubles, Venus runs a thousand ways; in the sweet and fatal warfare of desire, she is both the hunter and the hunted.

The law of nature is lawful marriage, and a wedding is the moment at which a woman takes the law into her own hands. "Believe then," Rosalind says, the day before she arranges four weddings, "that I can do strange things." There are accidents of confusion, shipwreck, and disguise, but these are only charming accompaniments to the vicissitudes of courtship. The women remain constant in their purpose; or else their mistakes are a part of the Goddess Nature's gentle domestic design:

> So comes it, lady, you have been mistook.
> But nature to her bias drew in that.

In *A Midsummer Night's Dream,* the moon, the emblem of change in the natural world, watches over nothing more dangerous than the midnight changes in the wood and the sad events by the Wall. The seasons, Titania says, are unnaturally altered; but in the comic vision this means only that between Titania and her husband there is a domestic quarrel:

> And this same progeny of evils comes
> From our debate, from our dissension;
> We are their parents and original.

Bottom, in the person of Pyramus, utters the *cri du coeur* of the tragic hero at the discovery of natural evil: "O, wherefore, Nature, didst thou lions frame?" But the lions of the comedies are harmless, their part is nothing but roaring, and Bottom rises from the dead to inquire: "Will it please you to see the Epilogue?" The events are directed by an art beyond the events; the comic design accomplishes its purpose in the face of any obstacle, and the epilogue is a blessing of the family, the woman's world fulfilled:

> So shall all the couples three
> Ever true in loving be;
> And the blots of Nature's hand
> Shall not in their issue stand.

If the Goddess Nature can blot her writing, what is it that jiggles her arm? No one asks; there is no mistake that cannot be crushed with the great plot of marriage. The Goddess Nature draws lovers to her bias, a grand and ancient dowager obliging the men to join the ladies.

II

To be ourselves, in the vision of comedy, is to realize a perfect idea of ourselves, and return to our original natural goodness. The Forest of Arden, in *As You Like It,* is like the golden world; it is a natural persuasion that leads us first to ourselves and then, in the happy notion of comedy, to one another. The Forest is not a natural paradise; there is winter and rough weather in it; but it is a picture of order that addresses the Duke Senior to teach him "what I am," and the shepherd Corin, who has lived in the Forest all his life, is a "natural philosopher" — though it is Touchstone who says so, and to be a natural philosopher is to be something of a fool.

Rosalind needs no instruction in who she is or whom she will marry; it is the women of comedy who by their own natural philosophy arrange the happy endings. But Orlando and Oliver are instructed in nature, and like the Duke Senior they are taught to know and to be themselves. At the beginning Orlando complains that his brother Oliver denies him any education; Orlando would be "a gentleman," he speaks of "gentility," the "gentle condition of blood," and "gentlemanlike qualities." Gentleness, he thinks, has been kept from him; but his brother Oliver confesses in puzzled hatred: "Yet he's gentle; never school'd and yet learned." Orlando has a natural gentleness, and when he enters the Forest his natural education is completed. The Forest at first seems a desert, the air seems bleak, and he advances upon the Duke Senior with a drawn sword; but the Duke tells him: "Your gentleness shall force," and when Orlando replies abashed: "I thought that all things had been savage here," the Duke bids him sit down "in gentleness." Pacing through the woods, Orlando comes upon Oliver asleep beside a lioness. Orlando might have turned away, but nature addresses him with the lesson of affection:

> Twice did he turn his back and purpos'd so;
> But kindness, nobler ever than revenge,
> And nature, stronger than his just occasion,
> Made him give battle to the lioness,
> Who quickly fell before him.

Orlando's gentleness, as it was before, is his by nature; his goodness, like the goodness of trees and stones and running brooks, is natural. And Oliver, who before was the "most un-natural" brother among men, is no longer what he was; he has become himself:

> 'Twas I. But 'tis not I! I do not shame
> To tell you what I was, since my conversion
> So sweetly tastes, being the thing I am.

The Forest has taught them who they are, and they are ready to be married.

The Forest is not perfect, and in *As You Like It* there are adverse judgments of the world. Orlando, pinning poems on every tree, attaches some that tell

> how brief the life of man
> Runs his erring pilgrimage.

But on the fairest boughs he will write "Rosalinda." The comic vision can permit touches of sorrow in a world capable of arranging a natural happiness that so far transcends them. When Rosalind exclaims: "O, how full of briers is this working-day world!" Celia answers: "They are but burrs, cousin, thrown upon thee in holiday foolery." The comic vision is a holiday of the fancy that repudiates from the start the more pressing and dangerous natural adversities. Comedy accepts the penalty of Adam into the Forest of Arden, admitting imperfection into a world assured to be more good than bad; and whatever cannot be shaped to fit the vision is happily disregarded. For the end of *As You Like It,* no matter what happens, will be marriage, a moment whose natural perfection is so certain that Touchstone, adjuring Audrey to bear her body more seeming, does no more than demonstrate how wide an area the moment of natural perfection embraces. Shallow villains and sleeping lions fall quickly before it; enemies are sweetly converted to themselves; and even heaven is glad:

> Then is there mirth in heaven
> When earthly things made even
> Atone together.

Hymen remarks, of the simultaneous union of eight people, that these are "strange events." They are indeed; but comedy, like Rosalind, can do strange things. The natural perfection of marriage disarms adversity, and finally adversity disarms itself. The Duke Senior and his men find their lands and fortune restored, and, to our philosophic dismay, they take it: they return to the envious court as joyfully as they had commended their absence from it. The artificial court and the natural Forest turn out, in the best of all possible worlds, not to be opposites after all; the choice ends in the pleasant discovery that both the fact and the dream can be had at once. Jaques's seven ages of man are a "strange eventful history," but in *As You Like It* they are a history that breaks off with an unconquerably happy ending.

III

There is comedy, like the comedy of Ben Jonson, that discovers and offers to our ridicule the disparity between the dream and the fact. Shakespearian comedy is more generous: it ends in the moment when fact is transformed into a dream, and when persons and things, at the ceremony of marriage, take their places in a formal image. The comedies come to terms with the two aspects of natural life by gathering things in themselves into a moment of timeless perfection. The end of Book I of *The Faerie Queene,* the betrothal of Una and the Red Cross Knight, is a picture of the establishment of perfect happiness; at the celebration there is "an heavenly noise."

Bacon had a rather different opinion of marriage: "He that hath wife and children hath given hostages to fortune; for they are impediments to great enterprises, either of virtue or mischief." Marriage is no impediment to the great enterprise of comedy; but what Bacon says in his judgment of poetry applies most justly to comic art. The art arranges the events, things submit to the dream, and there is in the vision "a more ample greatness, a more exact goodness, and a more absolute variety, than can be found in the nature of things." The comic vision is not responsible to natural fact, but in the Forest of Arden, in Bacon's words, "may at pleasure join that which nature hath severed, and sever that which nature hath joined." Comedy announces its own truth, that the truest poetry, as Touchstone says, is the most feigning, and that lovers are given to poetry. Comedy is true to its fancy: by an act of imagination it declares a happy ending in spite of fact. It is not the characters, but the vision itself, that is announced in the face of the world.

Only when the lovers have left the stage is there a hint of natural sadness: when Feste sings of the wind and the rain, and that a great while ago the world began, or when Robin Goodfellow reminds us that what has happened on the stage is no more than a dream. There are some facts that will not submit to the comic vision. Not everyone is married; the melancholy Jaques is never quite laughed out of existence. At the end he retreats into seclusion, withdrawing from a world that others have found sweet. He is not altogether a voice of comedy; he is a figure of dissent from the comic vision, who cannot be brought to agree that the purpose of natural life is matrimony. He is an intruder at a holiday who refuses to celebrate: "your experience makes you sad." The comic vision accepts his presence and at the end permits him to retire, undamaged by felicity. Only fools and Jaques stand apart from the continuance of the comic world; even Touchstone marries in his fashion. And Jaques refuses to be silent. He stands aside from the progress of society and announces who he is in despite of it. The fool is not in progress toward himself, the fool is always himself, and he preserves what he is by ignoring a world rushing headlong toward weddings. The fool is a fact, and he is the only fact that cannot be governed by the comic dream. Bottom and Dogberry and Jaques and Sir Andrew Aguecheek cannot alter the march of society; but they are able to step out of its way, and this ability wins them a peculiarly large share of our secret affections and admiration: only the fool can withstand the comic arrangement and dodge the slings and arrows of happiness; he is the reminder that the moment of perfection realized by the comic dream is only pretending.

So Falstaff is the fool of the history plays. He steps out of the way of English history, an intruder who announces himself in the face of the commonwealth; and in Falstaff the idea of order meets its most dangerous fact.

IV

At the beginning of *Henry* v, Exeter and Canterbury look toward the dream of an ordered commonwealth:

> For government, though high, and low, and lower,
> Put into parts, doth keep in one consent,
> Congreeing in a full and natural close,
> Like music.

31

> True! Therefore doth heaven divide
> The state of man in divers functions,
> Setting endeavor in continual motion;
> To which is fixed as an aim or butt
> Obedience; for so work the honeybees,
> Creatures that by a rule in nature teach
> The act of order to a peopled kingdom.

The natural order is a suggestion toward social order; the continuance of the natural world addresses society to persuade it toward its original perfection. The hope of society is that England may once more be "This other Eden, demi-paradise," or that France may be again "this best garden of the world." Society is endeavoring to return to what it was before, and to its first naturalness.

The image of perfect order shapes the events. But it stands apart from the events; it is made known through rhetorical speeches and formal interruptions. There is no reason for Exeter and Canterbury to speak of order — they are not talking to each other, and they are hardly listening to each other. They are speaking to us and explaining the splendid formula that governs their play, an idea that must be kept at a remove from the events of human incoherence. At the mid-point of *Richard* ii, a Gardener and his Servants trim the garden: he seems, to a weeping Queen, to be "old Adam's likeness," and his garden is a picture of the commonwealth in its original wholeness; in the garden there is "law and form and due proportion," and it shows, "as in a model, our firm estate." The garden is an emblem, like the Garden of Adonis in *The Faerie Queene*; and the scene itself is an emblematic episode in the history of a divided state and a deposed king. It is a moment of solace in the midst of disorder, a still center in a story of distress. The dream of order is unshaken by the debate and compromise of history; it persists through stories of revolt and flying-off; but it is a dream that can never be realized in fact. The subject of the histories is the continuing unrest of history, the magnificence of public tournaments and the hectic excitements of concealed plots; we look, as "in a theatre," at "industrious scenes and acts of death." In their sorrow and despair, revolting lords invoke the death of order:

> Let heaven kiss earth! Now let not Nature's hand
> Keep the wild flood confin'd! Let order die!

Above their heads the hand of the Goddess Nature, that in the comedies lays the red and white on a girl's face, is never relaxed; order is preserved. But there are facts in history which cannot be dismissed as readily as they are in the Forest of Arden; the image of order watches over the events, but the events themselves are a record of disorder.

There is a recurrent situation in the history plays: it is the exchange of speeches before a battle, when two opposing armies announce themselves, addressing each other with challenge and reply, and neither is altogether right or wrong. It is a situation that cannot be resolved; and it is repeated in the impossible dilemmas of single persons. "I know not what to do," York says; "Both are my kinsmen." And before a battle Blanch cries:

> Which is the side that I must go withal?
> I am with both; each army hath a hand,
> And in their rage, I having hold of both,
> They whirl asunder and dismember me.
> Husband, I cannot pray that thou mayst win;
> Uncle, I needs must pray that thou mayst lose;
> Father, I may not wish the fortune thine;
> Grandam, I will not wish thy wishes thrive.
> Whoever wins, on that side shall I lose;
> Assured loss before the match be play'd!

Single persons are divided, and their situation is written large in civil war, the "unkind division" that dismembers society itself, when sons and fathers kill each other and the times are "unnatural." It is an underlying perception of the history plays that men's claims on one another can never be resolved, that whichever wins there is assured loss, and that history is an argument made occasionally glorious by victories and coronations, but more often an uneasy bargain between irreconcilable opposites. The dream and the fact can never be brought together; and the impossible situation of their encounter is figured in the confrontation of Prince Hal and Falstaff.

In Prince Hal is expressed the vision of character and society in progress toward the dream. Society is reaching toward itself; character, within the continuance of society, is reaching toward itself; and both of these progressions are represented in Prince Hal. At the beginning of *The First Part of Henry* IV, he remains alone on the stage to announce who he is. He tells us, rather, who he will become: he will repudiate Falstaff, and like the sun he will please "again to be himself." He is a truant at Eastcheap; with Falstaff he only plays the part of the king his father. But he is in progress toward himself, and when he is made king he says to Falstaff: "Presume not that I am the thing I was." He is more than the thing he was, but not more than himself; he has redeemed the time and is himself again. He tries on his father's crown "as with an enemy," but the crown is an image of society's continuance, and by his wearing of it Prince Hal becomes himself indeed, the perfect image of an English king. Through the "noble change that I have purposed," Prince Hal and society realize the dream.

But Falstaff stands apart. Falstaff, not the crown, is the enemy; he is the figure of dissent from the vision of the play. He is indestructible, and the more so for being casual — rebellion lay in his way, as Falstaff says of someone else, and he found it. Falstaff is the fact of ordinary experience, and of our deep attachment to persons and things in themselves;

he is the sum of ordinary facts that stand in the road of the dream, a sum made extraordinary by its residence in one ancient body. Falstaff and the dream of order carry on at odds, in alternate scenes, and when they are brought face to face the vision of the play is unable to settle the dispute between such mighty opposites. In their encounter, the vision of the play confronts its own impossible dilemma: it is committed to both the fact of Falstaff and the dream of kingship. The repudiation of Falstaff is a moment that generations of spectators have found dramatically unsatisfactory; when Falstaff turns away to confess to Master Shallow, in that sudden access of honesty, that he owes him a thousand pound, it is a defeat too affecting to be endured. Falstaff cannot be repudiated; so real a fact cannot be dismissed; to banish plump Jack is to "banish all the world." He returns, like Bottom, in an epilogue: the story will be continued "with Sir John in it." He is put aside, but he returns, determined, as it were, to die of his own accord.

Yet Prince Hal does banish him; and in the play it is right that this is so. Prince Hal is not acting from causes within his character; the causes are within his public character, and what he is to become. He is acting under the impulsion of the idea of society and ourselves that directs the play, and it is the idea that triumphs and the fact of Falstaff that fades into a dream:

> I have long dreamt of such a kind of man,
> So surfeit-swell'd, so old, and so profane;
> But being awak'd, I do despise my dream.

Fact is repudiated, as it is in the Forest of Arden, to make possible a perfect image. The night before the battle of Agincourt, Prince Hal, become Henry v, thinks of the price his father paid in compassing the crown. He himself has paid a greater price by repudiating Falstaff; but the vision of the play, to realize itself, must indeed "banish all the world."

After the battle, Harry of England and Katherine of France are betrothed, like the lovers of comedy, or Una and the Red Cross Knight. In the widest sense, the story of Prince Hal and the crown is the story of comedy, and the vision of the history plays is a comic vision. Persons and events are made part of a plan moving toward perfection; things in themselves are transformed into an image of the further aspect of nature, its order and continuance. The vision of both the comedies and the histories belongs to the effort of the mind toward certainty and conclusion. The great plans of Bacon and Spenser, in this widest sense, belong to the same argument of hope; their vision is the vision of comedy. The endeavor toward certainty is an attempt to reach a settlement with the world that is contained in a single and absolute commitment; it is an endeavor toward the perfect shape of truth, and toward the recovery of an original wholeness in which fact is gathered into an arrangement that transfigures it. This great endeavor of the human spirit is what Bacon proposed when he looked toward the restoration of our knowledge to its perfect and original condition; it is the hope that informs Spenser's and Dante's vision of a divine comedy. It is one way of resolving what is within time and what is outside time, and one answer to the question, "What shall we do to be saved?"

v

Shortly after *Hamlet*, Shakespeare wrote the three problem comedies, *Troilus and Cressida, All's Well That Ends Well,* and *Measure for Measure*. A different resolution of the image and the fact is made known in the problem plays, and the difference is as great as any in Shakespeare's work.

The two subjects of *Troilus and Cressida* are war and love, the subjects of the histories and comedies; but *Troilus and Cressida* ends without victory, and without a wedding. Ulysses' speech on degree is not unlike the words of the Gardener in

Richard II or of Exeter and Canterbury in *Henry* v; it is an eloquent intrusion of discourse into the unrest of wartime, and its proposition is that the rules of nature teach the act of order to society. But Ulysses makes known how far the image of order has been lost and disregarded. His speech is not a dream of an order that can be recovered and that society is reaching toward; it is a discovery of the extent to which the Greeks have forfeited the dream. It is a disclosure of fact, a report of defeat beyond repair, a formal counterpart to Thersites' discovery of a general sickness:

> Most wisely hath Ulysses here discover'd
> The fever whereof all our power is sick.

In the corresponding Trojan council Hector proposes the moral laws of nature and of nations:

> Nature craves
> All dues be rend'red to their owners. Now
> What nearer debt in all humanity
> Than wife is to the husband? If this law
> Of nature be corrupted through affection,
> And that great minds, of partial indulgence
> To their benumbed wills, resist the same,
> There is a law in each well-ord'red nation
> To curb those raging appetites that are
> Most disobedient and refractory.
> If Helen then be wife to Sparta's king
> (As it is known she is), these moral laws
> Of nature and of nations speak aloud
> To have her back return'd.

The laws of nature and society address us; but four lines later Hector acquiesces in their neglect:

> Thus to persist
> In doing wrong extenuates not wrong,
> But makes it much more heavy. Hector's opinion
> Is this in way of truth. Yet ne'ertheless,

> My sprightly brethren, I propend to you
> In resolution to keep Helen still.

Ulysses' speech is acted out; the image of order is forfeited before our eyes. It is a painful moment, when it is confessed that a mind can go one way in truth and another in resolution. What is made known in *Troilus and Cressida* is a general sickness, the fever when degree is shaked, when the string is untuned, the will benumbed, and the image of order known but disobeyed. It is the dream that is surrendered to the fact; the image of order stands over what takes place, but it is powerless to shape the events.

The Duke in *Measure for Measure* speaks of nature as an unchanging moral law that addresses us with a demand for excellence:

> Spirits are not finely touch'd
> But to fine issues; nor Nature never lends
> The smallest scruple of her excellence
> But, like a thrifty goddess, she determines
> Herself the glory of a creditor,
> Both thanks and use.

But it seems to Isabella that a man, judged as he is in fact, is miserably impoverished:

> How would you be
> If he which is the top of judgment should
> But judge you as you are?

Natural man, without the gift of grace, plays such fantastic tricks before high heaven as make the angels weep; a man has a "natural guiltiness," and our natures, Claudio says, draw us toward evil:

> Our natures do pursue,
> Like rats that ravin down their proper bane,
> A thirsty evil, and when we drink we die.

Claudio would live; beseeching his sister, he tells her that natural affection will condone her fault:

> Sweet sister, let me live!
> What sin you do to save a brother's life,
> Nature dispenses with the deed so far
> That it becomes a virtue.

But to live may be the worst natural evil; the Duke tells Claudio to be "absolute for death," and the Duke's lesson, like the moral of a medieval *De contemptu mundi*, is the worthlessness of human nature and natural life.

The persons of *Measure for Measure* propose ideals of behavior. The Duke, or so he says, would have Claudio absolute for death; Angelo is absolute for justice; and Isabella, a maid whose mind is dedicate to nothing temporal, would be absolute for heaven. But a perfect image of conduct is not possible; the persons of the play are educated in natural fact. The Duke is put out of countenance by the prisoner Barnardine, a voice of dissent who refuses to be silent. Barnardine is absolute for life: "I will not consent to die this day, that's certain." He enters his cell or departs from it with equal composure, serenely unconscious, so far as can be seen, of the judgment passed upon him but never executed. Angelo is absolute for justice and Isabella for heaven: they also learn that their judgments are too precise. They are instructed in nature, like the characters of the comedies; but they cry out at their discovery of natural frailty. "O you beast!" cries Isabella, when Claudio would live; it is her moment of recognizing natural weakness in a brother. "O, fie, fie, fie!" cries Angelo, with Hamlet's expression of nausea, standing alone to announce himself with horror: "What dost thou? or what art thou, Angelo?" It is his discovery of natural evil in his thoughts and in the very fact of his birth, the "strong and swelling evil" of his "conception." It is a discovery that divides and paralyzes the mind: "we would, and we would not."

39

In every play there is a moment of discovery and *anagnorisis*, when character and event stand self-exposed. In the histories and comedies, it is the moment when lovers remove their disguises and are recognized. There are only touches of natural adversity in the histories and comedies, and only a few facts that cannot be gathered into the image of perfection: fools, who refuse to be married, and Falstaff, who refuses to be a member of an orderly commonwealth. Yet Falstaff and the idea of English kingship foreshadow the tragic collision between the fact and the image; the vision of the play is unable to cope with their encounter. The problem plays accept as their explicit theme the contradiction between these two aspects of experience: Ulysses and Hector and the Duke and Isabella are made to know and confront the fact of common natural weakness. At their most dramatic moments, they find themselves in a double situation, addressed by the world both as it is and as it ought to be. These are moments of intellectual anguish, when Angelo is torn between would and would not, and Isabella is at war " 'twixt will and will not." The cries of the lovers are discoveries that the dream of perfection and the fact of imperfection are bitterly divorced; they are cries not of the heart but of the mind: "this is, and is not, Cressid!"

VI

Nature is spoken of more often in *All's Well That Ends Well* than in any of the plays except *Hamlet* and *King Lear*. The demand that nature makes, as it is in the Forest of Arden, is love, and the continuance of society. It is not politic, Parolles tells Helena, to preserve virginity "in the commonwealth of nature." Virginity is "against the rule of nature" and "should be buried in highways out of all sanctified limit, as a desperate offendress against nature." Announcing the great message of comedy, Parolles says: "Get thee a good husband, and use him as he uses thee."

But nature is sick: the French nobility are "sick" for exploits, the younger of their "nature" go to war for "physic," and the "nature" of Parolles "sickens" to tell the truth. The French King is dying, and in him

> Nature and sickness
> Debate it at their leisure.

He cannot be cured by human art:

> The congregated college have concluded
> That labouring art can never ransom nature
> From her inaidable estate.

To Touchstone love seems a pleasant natural accident: "We that are true lovers run into strange capers; but as all is mortal in nature, so is all nature in love mortal in folly." But Bertram has "sick desires," Helena's eye is "sick on't," and when the Countess asks her fool the reason he will marry, the fool answers: "My poor body, madam, requires it. I am driven on by the flesh; and he must needs go that the devil drives." He has been "a wicked creature, as you and all flesh and blood are, and indeed I do marry that I may repent."

The debate of love is grown more perplexed. Helena would marry Bertram, she is as determined as Rosalind, but in Bertram there is a moral sickness: he "corrupts a well-derived nature" and is guilty of a "Natural rebellion." As nature and sickness debate in the King, the "blood and virtue" of Bertram contend "for empire." Bertram refuses to be married; he is in revolt against the continuance of society; in Bertram the figure of dissent is made the hero. It is Helena, like Rosalind, who must arrange a happy ending, but more serious demands are made of her. She must cure the King's natural sickness and Bertram's natural rebellion; and what

Bertram refuses is not the ceremony of marriage but its essential fact. Helena and Bertram are wedded before the end of the second act: Bertram rejects the "great prerogative and rite of love." He "will not bed her." He will not be called husband until she can show him a child of hers that he is father to. This is what Helena must accomplish to make complete the woman's world, the family; she must wear his ring and feel within her "her young one kick."

The comedies written before *Hamlet* bring their lovers to the ceremony of a wedding, and in the ceremony there is represented the image of formal order. In the problem plays the relations between men and women are more complicated; there is a more difficult agreement to be reached in love. There is a concern with sex, the most natural of all love's demands: Troilus and Cressida come together only in bed; sex is the argument between Angelo and Isabella, and between Helena and Bertram; and the language of the problem plays suggests the fever and intensity that accompany the act of love. The remedy, in *All's Well* and *Measure for Measure*, is a bed-trick. The plays have been criticized on this account; yet in some sense their subject is the trick of the bed. Their progress is toward the deeply perplexing moment in natural experience when without order or ceremony the woman's world is consummated in fact, a moment not of simple joy and natural perfection, but of the peculiar anguish of joy and pain at once.

The two strains of Elizabethan thought that are associated with Hooker and Calvin, and in drama with Chapman and Webster, come to different estimates of what is natural in ourselves. There is something of this difference in what is said about the natural self in the histories and comedies and in the problem plays. The characters of the histories and comedies learn the lesson of *The French Academy*, that "There is nothing more true, than that nature of hir-selfe leadeth men in some sort to that which is decent and honest," or the lesson of Cicero's *De Officiis*: "nature, whom if we wil folow as guide, we shall never go amisse." Adam and Eve made the first marriage, and it was a picture of natural perfection; the histories and comedies look back to that original integrity, to old Adam's likeness, to another Eden, and to the golden world. Certainly in the histories and comedies the purposes of conduct and of art are "to know Nature and to follow her." Their vision looks back to the first event in the Christian history of nature, its creation, when God saw everything that he had made, and it was good.

But the more Augustinian judgment of natural character is that "naturally," as Calvin said, "wee are all sycke of one desease." It was Adam and Eve who made the first revolt; and the vision of the problem plays includes this second event in the Christian history of nature, the Fall, which "perverted the whole order of nature in Heaven and in Earth." This pessimism is felt in the plays of Webster or Marston or Tourneur; and it is expressed by Spenser when he finds the world to be run quite out of square, moving toward its dissolution and its last ruinous decay. The original heresy, William Perkins said, is "naturally ingrafted in mans nature," we receive from Adam a "naturall inclination onely to conceive and devise the thing which is evil," our will "naturally is a flat bondslave unto sinne," and one of the false guides of life is "the light of naturall reason." Original sin, in the words of the Thirty-Nine Articles, is "the fault and corruption of the Nature of every man, that naturally is ingendred of the offspring of Adam; whereby man is very far gone from original righteousness, and is of his own nature inclined to evil." Thus we have heard, it was preached according to the Homilies, "howe evil we be of our selves, howe of our selves and by our selves, we have no goodnes, helpe, nor salvacion, but contrarywise, synne, dampnacion, and death everlastyng."

43

The characters of the problem plays, like the persons of Arden or Eastcheap, are taught to know themselves; but they are pained and dismayed by what they discover. Parolles puts his trust in what he is in himself: "Simply the thing I am," he announces, "Shall make me live." Parolles is a rascal. And a First and Second Lord tell us what we are in ourselves. "Now God delay our rebellion! As we are ourselves, what things are we!" To which the other Lord replies: "Merely our own traitors." *Measure for Measure* and *All's Well* end in marriage; but all is not well at the ending; the judgments of ourselves and society have been too severe. When the Duke says that "a remedy presents itself," we are involved once more in the plot of matrimony, and when he takes Isabella by the hand, the catastrophe is still a nuptial. But these are marriages with a difference: we have been made aware of matters too serious to be concluded so patly, with the catastrophe of the old comedy. Helena and the Duke must manipulate too many events and shape too many lives; and there is no simple delight about their art, as there is about Rosalind's, and no magic, as there is in Prospero's. There is something disappointing and unsuccessful about the weddings they arrange; the conclusions of *Measure for Measure* and *All's Well* are not moments of natural perfection, but acknowledgements of a natural weakness of blood and desire that must somehow be compromised with. Affairs must be patched up; some cure must be found; an agreement of some kind must be made with natural fact, or a temporary armistice.

When Prince Hal says to Falstaff, "I know thee not, old man," then by his saying so even the fact of Falstaff disappears. We know or do not know Falstaff, according to the will of the comic vision; but there is knowledge in the problem plays that cannot be put aside. "Truth is truth," Isabella says bravely, "To th' end of reck'ning." But at the end she kneels to beg mercy for Angelo's falseness. Isabella, a thing enskied and sainted, who condemned her brother's natural fault as absolutely as Angelo, learns that there are no absolutes in natural life, and that truth, as she said at first to Angelo, is "set down so in heaven, but not in earth." In her kneeling a perfect image is relinquished: perfect justice is surrendered to give place to mercy, and her own perfect sanctity surrenders itself to a wedding. The characters of the problem plays discover the world, in Bacon's phrase, such as it is in fact, not such as a man's own reason would have it to be. They act knowingly, and it is their knowledge that perplexes them; they act and believe and are married in spite of what they know.

VII

There is a suggestion in the problem plays of religious possibilities that answer this sense of the incompleteness of natural things in themselves. Spenser explained that the first two of his *Four Hymns* were "of earthly or naturall love and beautie," and the second two "of heavenly and celestiall." A distinction of the same sort can be made between the histories and comedies and the problem plays. In *Measure for Measure* and *All's Well*, a remedy is proposed for the sickness and guilt of natural character that is not required in the Forest of Arden: it is suggested that we may, by knowing ourselves, become more than ourselves, and that our commerce with one another may be natural and heavenly at once, sanctifying error.

There is religious reference in the histories and comedies; it would be surprising if there were not. Old religious men wander at the outskirts of the Forest of Arden, like a fringe, as Rosalind might have said, but did not, on a natural petticoat. But it is in the plays that follow, *Hamlet* and *All's Well* and *Measure for Measure*, that religious possibilities are for the first time a serious concern of Shakespeare's art; or it was

45

in these plays that his art acquired sufficient assurance to suggest what had always been a concern. Part of the greater seriousness of *Measure for Measure* is that the agent of social justice, who once was Dogberry and his minions, is now the Duke; and part of this same seriousness is that the Duke is disguised as a friar and that his devices seem religious. What makes Angelo ask forgiveness is a sense of heaven's watching presence:

> I perceive your Grace, like pow'r divine,
> Hath look'd upon my passes.

And what makes mercy possible is a sense of heaven's forgiveness:

> Why, all the souls that were were forfeit once,
> And he that might the vantage best have took
> Found out the remedy.

There is a more than natural remedy for the forfeiting of ourselves.

So Helena finds out a cure for natural sickness and rebellion. The remedy is love; but love may be religious. The Countess' fool will marry because his poor body requires it, but he has "other holy reasons." Bertram says that his love is "holy," and the King that it should be "religious." Helena's eye is "sick," but her fancy is heavenly:

> But now he's gone, and my idolatrous fancy
> Must sanctify his relics.

She loves Bertram "next unto high heaven," and is "Religious in mine error." "What angel," the Countess asks, will "Bless this unworthy husband?" The answer is Helena, who cures the King and redeems Bertram. The King's natural sickness is inaidable by natural means, but Helena tells him: "Of heaven, not me, make an experiment." Her father was a physician of such skill that he could almost have "made nature immortal." She has learned her father's art, and she will cure the King with the "great'st grace lending grace." She is, it seems, "undoubted blest." Lafew says in awe:

> They say miracles are past, and we have our philosophical persons, to make modern and familiar, things supernatural and causeless. Hence it is that we make trifles of terrors, ensconcing ourselves into seeming knowledge when we should submit ourselves to an unknown fear.

"Gentlemen," Helena tells the court, "Heaven hath through me restor'd the King to health." She is a woman:

> I am a simple maid, and therein wealthiest
> That I protest I simply am a maid.

But she is a woman who is the natural instrument of heaven. Her cure is the

> Very hand of heaven —
> Ay, so I say.
> In a most weak —
> And debile minister, great power, great transcendence.

Her remedy is a "showing of a heavenly effect in an earthly actor."

It may be that Shakespeare took this theme from a hint by Helena's original, Giletta of Narbonne in *The Palace of Pleasure*, who said: "I do not minister Phisicke by profession, but by the aide and helpe of God." Certainly this theme occupied Shakespeare's mind in *Measure for Measure* and *All's Well*; in *Troilus and Cressida* there is no sense of heaven, and no marriage. There is a mysterious power about the Duke and Helena, and it is through this power that they arrange events. Helena follows Bertram to Italy as a pilgrim of St. Jaques — as if the peevish figure of the Forest of Arden had unexpectedly been canonized — and finds in Diana another instrument of heaven:

47

> Doubt not but heaven
> Hath brought me up to be your daughter's dower,
> As it hath fated her to be my motive
> And helper to a husband.

Parolles and Helena debate for the possession of Bertram; they are the opposites in the argument of the play between nature and virginity, sickness and health, blood and virtue, and nature and grace. Parolles is unmasked as a coward, and Helena is masked in bed. At Rossillion, at home, a gentle Helena and a bewildered Bertram confront each other; it is the moment of recognition, in which Helena, like Rosalind, reveals herself. She is not dead, she is alive, and Diana says:

> Dead though she be, she feels her young one kick.
> So there's my riddle: one that's dead is quick —
> And now behold the meaning.

"O, pardon!" cries Bertram; it is the word that Isabella kneels for. Helena's folktale duties have been accomplished; sickened and rebellious nature has been brought to health and marriage; and it is suggested that this has been done with a more than secular assistance.

VIII

But it remains no more than a suggestion. We cannot think of *Measure for Measure* as an analogue of the Christian story of the atonement; Shakespeare's mind does not move in this manner. The religious possibilities that touch Helena and the Duke, as Diana says, are a "riddle." In Helena's curing of the King and in her pregnancy there are odd reminders of the curing of the Fisher King and the restoration of his land to fertility. But Shakespeare's mind does not move in this way either; his meanings are simpler and more obscure. When Diana says, "And now behold the meaning," she is announcing no more than the entrance of Helena. It is the human figure of Helena who both proposes the riddle and answers it; she is in herself the most complete statement that the play makes; she is the meaning. Even in the problem plays, Shakespeare's most intellectual exercises, his imagination is engaged to persons and things: Helena is a simple maid, "the most virtuous gentlewoman that ever nature had praise for creating," a woman feeling her young one kick. She is also, or so it seems, "the herb of grace." She suggests that the actions of a human being may share in a larger action; the two aspects of experience are joined within her, in an internal wedding. A human being, as Guillaume Du Vair said, is "the knot, the marriage knot which linketh heavenly & earthly things together."

In the histories and comedies the two aspects of the natural condition are the fact of natural incompleteness and the dream of natural order; the vision moves toward the moment of marriage or victory when fact is transformed and the dream is realized. In *All's Well* and *Measure for Measure* these two aspects of natural life are extended; character is poised between natural incompleteness and the dream of grace. The movement its toward a point at which character, while remaining itself, has the added possibility of sharing in what is beyond itself. In Helena and the Duke the vision of the problem plays arrives at its own reconciliation between time and what is beyond time and informing it; the figures of Helena and the Duke represent a second answer to the question of what we shall do to be saved. It is not an answer by which character and society are restored to their original natural integrity; it is an answer expressed finally in the vision of tragedy, where character stands alone between heaven and earth and shares in both. In the problem plays this reconciliation made within individual character is not always expressed successfully. *All's Well* has been called a failure and *Measure for Measure* a hybrid, and no doubt they are; it is no recommendation, certainly, to say that they are congenial to the modern temper. The problem plays, like the modern temper, are at war; the separation between things and meaning, that is suggested in the collision between Falstaff and the crown, is made explicit, and every resource of comedy is needed to repair it. The problem plays are divided between folktale and Christian symbol, between success and failure, and between comedy and tragedy. The contradiction between things and meaning belongs to tragedy, and the Duke speaks of a resolution no longer comic when he says: "Be absolute for death."

III

TRAGIC CHARACTER

There are only two women in *Hamlet,* and they are bewildered and forlorn, and unable to arrange a happy ending; *Hamlet* does not end with a wedding, it begins with a wedding, and Hamlet's word to his uncle is, "I say, we will have no more marriages." In tragedy we are made to see the fatal collision between the fact and the idea, and we witness the effort of human character to reach a settlement, without aid, between these two aspects of the natural situation. Tragic character defines itself through its own strength and in its solitary encounter with the tragic world. There is no sense in the tragic world of a continuance drawing personality toward a perfect image; there is instead another and more deadly persuasion, drawing character toward its own defeat, and it is against this persuasion that character endeavors to establish its identity and reach an agreement with the natural condition.

I should like to turn first to three tragedies that are set in Shakespeare's Mediterranean world: *Othello, Timon of Athens,* and *Coriolanus. Hamlet* and *King Lear* belong to a northern world of ghosts and storms, where the air is chill and cutting. But *Othello* and *Timon of Athens* and *Coriolanus* take place in the world of the comedies, a southern region of natural passions, local squalls, and personal calamity. The tragic encounter is restricted; there is a sense of claustrophobia, and of closeness and suffocation; the vision is circumscribed by what Bradley calls in *Othello* the "comparative confinement of the imaginative atmosphere." It is a vision not of character confronting the world, but of character encountering itself.

II

There are suggestions of wider meanings in *Othello*. Othello thinks of chaos come again, and he imagines a universal alteration of the natural world:

> Methinks it should be now a huge eclipse
> Of sun and moon, and that th' affrighted globe
> Should yawn at alteration.

But this is a dream, there is no eclipse, and the alteration and chaos come only to Othello himself. His words are not an extension of the meaning of the play; they are a shocking indication of the extent of his personal ruin. The "*Othello* music" is for a solo instrument; its sorrow, as Brabantio says, is not the general care but the particular grief; our concern is with Othello. The natural demands made upon Othello are the internal demands of blood and judgment:

> Now, by heaven,
> My blood begins my safer guides to rule,
> And passion, having my best judgment collied,
> Assays to lead the way.

His disposition is shaken not by the address of a ghost or a storm, but by natural passion:

> Nature would not invest herself in such shadowing passion without some instruction. It is not words that shakes me thus. — Pish! Noses, ears, and lips? Is't possible? — Confess? — handkerchief? — O devil!

TRAGIC CHARACTER

The balance of our lives, Iago says, has one scale of reason to poise another of sensuality; the power lies in our own wills, and it is in ourselves that we are thus or thus. Though these are Iago's words, they are a description of natural character that the events of the play suggest to be true; his description establishes, at the end of the first act, the vantage point from which natural character will be explored and studied. In *Richard* II a garden is an emblem of society; in *Hamlet* it is a metaphor for an unweeded world; but in the confinement of *Othello* a garden is a figure for individual human nature, a nature that is self-contained and self-explanatory, addressed by voices within itself, a combination of blood and judgment that includes its own causes of order and disorder.

In the southern tragedies we are made least aware of religious possibilities beyond the natural self. There are religious suggestions about Desdemona and Iago: the look in Desdemona's eyes can hurl a soul from heaven, while the heavenly shows of Iago are a divinity of hell, and at the end, as if he were a devil, he bleeds but is not killed. It is suggested that the "divine" Desdemona and the devilish Iago are counterparts, rivals for the possession of Othello who persuade him toward the opposite ends of love and jealousy, like the good and bad angels of a morality play, the good and bad counselors of a political play, or Helena and Parolles in *All's Well*, the rivals who debate the ownership of Bertram. But these are only scattered hints; they do not raise questions in our minds, nor are they explorations of an undiscovered country. What is asked of Othello, and of Timon of Athens and Coriolanus, is a balanced adjustment of the natural elements of themselves, their natural reason and natural passion. The adjustment is far from easy, but its importance is not in doubt; it is a problem uncomplicated by the disturbing religious awareness, suggested in *All's Well* and *Measure for Measure*, that any natural arrangement of the self is inade-

quate. Othello's failure is a natural failure, and he falls to
bestiality, not to damnation. It is not in the special providence
of a fallen sparrow, but in himself, that Othello is thus or
thus; he confronts his own character, and it is this encounter
that is driven to its extremity and that grows frightening by
reason of its confinement.

The vantage point of natural ethics is below the higher
ground of a severe religious judgment: to select it is to choose,
for the time being, a perspective in which the natural self is
regarded as a system containing its own sources of life and
motion. This is not to say that *Othello* is a Stoic play; Shakespeare's imagination is not attached to so precise a philosophy.
Yet the concerns of this southern world are those of the *De
Officiis*, self-knowledge, self-control, the rule of reason, the
instruction of universal nature, and the guidance of individual nature. "For in suche wise we muste worke," Othello and
Timon and Coriolanus learn too late, "as againste all nature
wee never strive: which thing avoided, let us folow our owne
proper nature." The vision of the plays is not naturalism;
Iago is the naturalist. Nor is it a denial of a religious vision.
But they are plays, like the histories and comedies, in which
a religious explanation is not necessary, as it is necessary in
All's Well and *Measure for Measure,* to make the events com-
prehensible. In the broadest sense, Shakespeare's southern
tragedies accept the terms of Bacon's natural philosophy: they
are explorations of natural character, of natural causes, and
of natural things in themselves.

III

In the histories and comedies, character alters to become
itself; princes and lovers are sweetly converted to what they
are. Orlando receives a natural education and a wife, and
when Prince Hal completes his "noble change," he becomes,
like Prince Arthur in *The Faerie Queene,* a perfect image of

a man. In the problem plays there are more serious discoveries, that the self is divided between what is and what is not itself, and character is converted by more drastic changes: when Bertram reads the letter from his mother that begins the cure of his natural rebellion, he is "chang'd almost into another man." The alteration of character into itself is described by religious language, like the conversions of personality that are effected by grace; to think of what we are in ourselves, Isabella tells Angelo, is to know our natural weakness, to learn mercy, and to be "Like man new made."

These are alterations by which character becomes itself or more than itself. Change in the tragic world is more ominous. It is a confounding of what is and is not ourselves; it brings danger to the natural arrangement of the self, and to a natural nobility already established. Before his father's death Hamlet is the perfect image of a prince, the expectancy and rose of the fair state, the observed of all observers; but in his "transformation" he is his mother's "too much changed son." In the tragic world, the alteration of character is a loss and a falling-off; it is part of Lear's pain to suffer

> These dispositions that of late transform you
> From what you rightly are.

Othello's character is known to the world; his life is already a story, a romance of battles, sieges, and disastrous chances. He has a "free and open nature," a "constant, loving, noble nature," a "good nature," and a "free and noble nature." He has a natural nobility; but a "noble nature," as Flavius says in *Timon of Athens*, may "catch a wrench." Othello's natural character is the source of his love and his jealousy, his success and his defeat. The natural self directs his existence; it makes existence possible; it is of such importance that a wrench is mortal, and an alteration of the self from its natural arrangement reduces human character to the level of the animals.

57

Othello protests that he will never obey the changes of the moon; he kneels to swear that he will be as constant as the icy current of the Pontic Sea; but Iago knows that Othello is already altered from what he rightly is:

> The Moor already changes with my poison.

Desdemona says in fear:

> My lord is not my lord; nor should I know him,
> Were he in favour as in humour alter'd.

"Exchange me for a goat," Othello cries. His heart is "turn'd to stone" — he strikes it, and it hurts his hand. "He is much chang'd," Iago says, and Emilia exclaims: "Here's a change indeed!" The language of change and alteration runs through the events: the messages to the Venetian council change by the minute, and Roderigo, dissuaded from drowning, announces: "I am chang'd." Cassio is flustered with wine, and cries out at the change that takes place not only in himself but in his general, the reduction of natural character to the level of the animals: "To be now a sensible man, by-and-by a fool, and presently a beast!"

Only Desdemona seems beyond change. The women of comedy remain constant, while their lovers vary in their desires; Rosalind arranges the four weddings in the Forest of Arden, Isabella kneels for Angelo, and Helena finds out the remedy for Bertram. So in the tragic world, Ophelia, if she could, would find a remedy for her lord; and Cordelia would bring restoration to her father. They stand in the way of the tragic progress; they would turn it aside; and Desdemona, if she were able, would set matters right between Othello and Cassio. She remains herself, moving in frightened but unaltered innocence, and in herself she is a perfect image, enwheeled around by grace. She is framed as fruitful as "the free elements," and like the world before the Fall, the first alteration and loss of natural integrity, she wears "th' essential vesture of creation." At her approach, it seems to Cassio that a sense of her beauty alters even the forces of the storm:

> Tempests themselves, high seas, and howling winds,
> The gutter'd rocks and congregated sands,
> Traitors ensteep'd to clog the guiltless keel,
> As having sense of beauty, do omit
> Their mortal natures, letting go safely by
> The divine Desdemona.

To let her pass by, the waves change their mortal natures; but it is not permitted to Desdemona to pass untouched through the personal storm of Othello's change. She too is implicated in the theme of alteration. Her father accuses Othello of beguiling her from herself:

> For nature so prepost'rously to err,
> Being not deficient, blind, or lame of sense,
> Sans witchcraft could not.

She must have been bewitched to go so contrary to all the rules of universal nature:

> and she — in spite of nature,
> Of years, of country, credit, everything —
> To fall in love with what she fear'd to look on!
> It is a judgment maim'd and most imperfect
> That will confess perfection so could err
> Against all rules of nature.

Iago assures Roderigo that she will change again:

> She must change for youth. When she is sated with his body, she will find the error of her choice. She must have change, she must.

The rules of nature itself will teach her change:

> Very nature will instruct her in it and compel her to some second choice.

Giraldi Cinthio's Disdemona confessed that her marriage with a Moor was against "la Natura." In the play it is the judgment of her father, of Iago, and of the altered Othello that is maimed and most imperfect, not her own; she has not turned from the rules of universal nature, and the witchcraft Othello used was a love that fulfilled and completed her nature. But Othello begins in doubt: "And yet, how nature erring from itself —" and Iago continues:

> Ay, there's the point! as (to be bold with you)
> Not to affect many proposed matches
> Of her own clime, complexion, and degree,
> Whereto we see in all things nature tends —
> Foh! one may smell in such a will most rank,
> Foul disproportion, thoughts unnatural.

She is accused of "disproportion," as the messages to the Venetian council were "disproportion'd." She has turned from her proper course of nature, as the alarm bell in Act II frighted the isle "From her propriety." She can alter, Othello says, endlessly:

> Sir, she can turn, and turn, and yet go on,
> And turn again.

IV

Desdemona has not changed; she is herself still; but at the end she suffers the ultimate natural alteration. She almost diverts Othello's mortal purpose: she can sing the savageness out of a bear, and as she sleeps she almost persuades Othello to break the sword of "Justice." Awake, she cries: "That death's unnatural that kills for loving." But Othello inflicts upon her the natural change that cannot be called back; he puts out the light, that cannot be relumed, in the "cunning'st pattern of excelling nature." If Brabantio could see his dead daughter, Gratiano says, the sight of her would make him do a desperate turn; but Brabantio is beyond change, he too is dead, and Othello kills himself before our eyes.

The end of *Othello* is the destruction of character and identity. Before his death Othello makes a last address to the world; he would make known the service he has done the state, and he would have those around him "Speak of me as I am." He would recover his identity and be himself again. And he is addressing more than those around him; he is making his voice heard to the world, to reëstablish his name beyond the moving accidents of his life. But there is much to be said for Mr. Eliot's judgment of this speech. It is not humility; it is bravado; Othello is "cheering himself up." He is adopting, Mr. Eliot says, "an *aesthetic* rather than a moral attitude, dramatising himself against his environment." The words and gestures with which Othello addresses his situation are an announcement of who he is. But they are without meaning; we might say, rephrasing Mr. Eliot, that the conclusion of *Othello* is most certainly a moral failure. Othello is too much altered from himself; he is "he that was Othello." In the heated and confined air of the play, the loss of self is the loss of country, credit, everything; there is nothing left, and Othello's last gesture is to strike at his own throat. The gesture is meaningless; and the play, Granville-Barker says, is "a tragedy without meaning, and that is the ultimate horror of it." There is personal defeat at the end of *Hamlet* and *King Lear*, but there is a suggestion that in defeat character may come to terms with what is beyond itself. No such suggestion is made at the end of *Othello*. Othello has reached no settlement with his world, except to leave it; there is nothing that character can do to be saved.

v

Timon of Athens and Coriolanus are altered from themselves; they are two more noble figures whose personal defeats are seen in the hard, clear light of the southern world.

Timon's "nature" is "good and gracious," but in Act IV he grubs for roots before a cave; he is "Transformed Timon." His servant Flavius laments his "alteration," and Alcibiades asks: "How came the noble Timon to this change?" It is a change in which Timon rejects the world. He is almost altered once more by Flavius, as Othello is almost changed by Desdemona; to remember his faithful servant "almost turns my dangerous nature mild." But he perseveres in his hatred of humanity and his "contempt of nature." His repudiation of the world is as confined a calamity as Othello's; the cause is the distortion of himself, and the imperfect judgment of his altered character. In the first three acts it is Apemantus who is, as a Lord gently remarks, "opposite to humanity." Apemantus is what Timon becomes; with nothing more to say in the last two acts, Apemantus sounds out of place and ill at ease. Even in the first three acts, though Apemantus and Timon are opposites, they are oddly drawn toward each other, as if they found a peculiar importance in each other's company. They go together, like the captain and the stowaway in Joseph Conrad's *The Secret Sharer*; they are, as it were, two aspects of a single self, the extremes between which the personality of a human being can alternate. The consequences of Timon's alteration are what Othello is reduced to, bestiality and death. A "contempt of nature" is a contempt of life; a denial of natural feeling is a rejection of one's existence as a human being, and finally of existence itself. Only at the end do Timon and Othello recognize the natural feeling they have extinguished: Othello acknowledges that he loved his wife, not wisely, but too well; and Timon builds his tomb on the shore of the sea, where the waves can weep for him. Alcibiades understands his intention:

> Though thou abhorr'dst in us our human griefs,
> Scorn'dst our brine's flow and those our droplets which

> From niggard nature fall, yet rich conceit
> Taught thee to make vast Neptune weep for aye
> On thy low grave, on faults forgiven.

At the end Timon preserves some part of his human kindness; and there is in Shakespeare's vision a measure of forgiveness for a denial of natural feeling that at length can wish to be remembered with natural sorrow.

Othello and Timon are turned toward jealousy and hatred; the alteration of Coriolanus is to mercy and kindness. Coriolanus has a natural nobility, but his character is fixed in pride; he seems beyond the order and continuance of nature:

> He leads them like a thing
> Made by some other deity than Nature,
> That shapes men better.

He is himself alone; his own nature seems separate from universal nature, as if it lived apart from its natural setting, sustained by its own force. His "nature" disdains the shadow which he treads on at noon; he is like an engine; he is like a god. He seems unalterable: his "nature" is "no changeling," and it is his "nature" not to be "other than one thing." He is the rock, the oak not to be wind-shaken, and his one friend can only say that "His nature is too noble for the world."

But at the end, at the supplication of his family, he is shaken with natural feeling, and bows his own nature to the demands of natural affection. In Act iii, Coriolanus asks:

> Would you have me
> False to my nature?

And his mother answers:

> I would dissemble with my nature where
> My fortunes and my friends at stake requir'd
> I should do so in honour.

63

At the end she would have him again be false to his nature, and obedient, instead, to natural feeling. The choice is between his own nature and universal nature; and Coriolanus makes a last declaration of his independence, addressing whatever distant audience listens to a human being when he chooses:

> But out, affection!
> All bond and privilege of nature, break!
> Let it be virtuous to be obstinate.
> What is that curtsy worth? or those dove's eyes,
> Which can make gods forsworn? I melt and am not
> Of stronger earth than others. My mother bows,
> As if Olympus to a molehill should
> In supplication nod; and my young boy
> Hath an aspect of intercession which
> Great nature cries "Deny not." — Let the Volsces
> Plough Rome and harrow Italy! I'll never
> Be such a gosling to obey instinct, but stand
> As if a man were author of himself
> And knew no other kin.

But his mother prevails; Coriolanus yields to natural feeling. "Is't possible," a Tribune inquires skeptically, "that so short a time can alter the condition of a man?" Coriolanus acknowledges the demands of nature's continuance; he is not a god, nor is he author of himself; he is made by no other deity than Nature, and he cannot live apart from the natural setting. He obeys instinct; he submits his own nature to the bond, privilege, and intercession of universal nature. As Plutarch puts it, Coriolanus is "overcome in the end with natural affection," and "nature so wrought with him, that the teares fell from his eyes, and he could not keepe himself from making much of them, but yeelded to the affection of his bloud, as if he had bene violently caried with the furie of a most swift running streame."

Coriolanus accepts what Timon and Othello refuse, natural

feeling; he bows himself to the continuance of things. His family, as Desdemona could not, persuade "Justice" to break its sword, and they are able, as Flavius was not, to turn a dangerous nature mild. But the irony of Coriolanus' submission of his character to the natural arrangement of the world is that this change too is fatal. His acceptance of the continuance of things is a repudiation of the fact of himself; his encounter with the world, like Othello's and Timon's, ends in the loss and defeat of personality. There is no settlement possible between himself and the world. His choice, like the choice that Prince Hal must make between Falstaff and the crown, is between things in themselves and the continuance that gives meaning to things; he is divided, like Angelo, between what he is and what he should be. The choice between the fact and the dream is one that Coriolanus cannot resolve. His mother has prevailed "Most dangerously." Her success will be "most mortal." The scene, he thinks, is "unnatural," and his part in it he cannot discharge to the life.

VI

In *Othello, Timon of Athens,* and *Coriolanus,* our encounter with the aspects of natural life is seen as an encounter with our own natures and with the larger natural arrangement of affection and pity. Bacon wrote that "Nature is often hidden; sometimes overcome; seldom extinguished." The tragic defeat of Othello and Timon and Coriolanus is the consequence of their extinguishing what is natural in themselves and their separation of themselves from the natural arrangement. They have a natural nobility; they are honorable men; but they reject natural feeling to commit themselves unnaturally to absolutes and to what seems to be the perfect shape of action and belief. "It is the cause, it is the cause," Othello says; he is dedicated, like Angelo, to what he thinks is an absolute justice beyond natural affection.

"The middle of humanity thou never knewest," Apemantus says to Timon, "but the extremity of both ends." Timon is committed first to one extreme and then to its opposite; and Coriolanus' mother tells her son: "You are too absolute." They are three absolutists, pledged to certainties and conclusions that are sadly mistaken. They repudiate their natural allegiance to the things of the world; they embrace pride, "Justice," or a "contempt of nature." They separate themselves from the world that gives them being, and the result is suicide and the death of the heart.

In *Macbeth* Shakespeare explores in a northern setting this loss of identity and division of character from the larger natural order. The suggestion of the Witches would have Macbeth go contrary to what is natural in himself; their soliciting

> doth unfix my hair
> And make my seated heart knock at my ribs
> Against the use of nature.

Natural feeling is what Lady Macbeth fears in her husband:

> Yet do I fear thy nature.
> It is too full o' th' milk of human kindness
> To catch the nearest way.

She would stop up natural pity in Macbeth, and deny it in herself:

> Come, you spirits
> That tend on mortal thoughts, unsex me here,
> And fill me, from the crown to the toe, top-full
> Of direst cruelty! Make thick my blood;
> Stop up th' access and passage to remorse,
> That no compunctious visitings of nature
> Shake my fell purpose nor keep peace between
> Th' effect and it!

Macbeth would hide their deed from the natural world:

> Come, thick night,
> And pall thee in the dunnest smoke of hell,
> That my keen knife see not the wound it makes,
> Nor heaven peep through the blanket of the dark
> To cry, "Hold, hold!"

He fears that nature will speak aloud:

> Thou sure and firm-set earth,
> Hear not my steps which way they walk, for fear
> Thy very stones prate of my whereabout.

For Macbeth is murdering nature:

> Now o'er the one half-world
> Nature seems dead.

He is taking life, "Nature's copy" and "the lease of nature." Duncan's two grooms are so drugged that their "drenched natures lie as in a death," and "death and nature do contend about them." Duncan's gashed stabs look like "a breach in nature," and Banquo is left by the Murderers with twenty wounds, the "least a death to nature."

Macbeth and his Lady are doing "nature's mischief," and though they would conceal what they do from the natural order, the world replies. On the night of Duncan's murder, there is storm and darkness; it is "unnatural," like "the deed that's done." A falcon is killed by a mousing owl, and Duncan's horses turn "wild in nature." At the end Birnam Wood comes to Dunsinane, and

> Unnatural deeds
> Do breed unnatural troubles.

These are the outward consequences of nature's mischief; and the internal fatality is the assassination of what is natural in the self. Macbeth has murdered sleep, "great nature's second course," and at the appearance of Banquo's Ghost he wonders how his wife can keep "the natural ruby" of her cheeks. For they have smothered natural feeling and human kindness; they have no longer "the natural touch." Lady Macbeth dies insane and Macbeth in despair; there is in both, as the Doctor says of Lady Macbeth's sleep-walking, a "great perturbation in nature." In his frenzy Macbeth would dare a universal confusion, the tumbling together of nature's germens; and when at the end he throws himself upon Macduff in an empty and terrible excitement, he is, as surely as Othello or Timon or Coriolanus, committing suicide.

The tragic vision concerns itself with different forms of evil; in Shakespeare's exploration of character divided from the world, his concern is with the evil of acting and believing without meaning. Iago does indeed move in motiveless malignity; he is evil because what he does has no reason, and the play itself ends "without meaning." There are motives given for Othello's jealousy, but it may be that they were better left out; Thomas Rymer said with some justice that the misplacing of the handkerchief is a warning to wives to look well to their linen. Leontes in *The Winter's Tale* suffers a more terrible and convincing onrush of jealousy, and it is convincing and terrible because it is senseless; there is no motive and no cause. What is terrible about Timon is his meaningless despair: "I care not." And we are cabined, cribbed, and confined by Macbeth's despair; the dreadful emptiness of what he does and thinks is extended throughout his world until the world becomes a projection of himself. When he is hailed by the Witches, his ambition is given a shape and voice that stops him on the road and greets him; he is made to hear the address of part of himself. The suggestion of the Witches is his own suggestion; it shakes his thought, that before was but fantastical, and in the encounter that character has with itself there is a quality of dread and alarm that makes Macbeth's seated heart knock at his ribs. The soliciting of the Witches cannot be ill, cannot be good;

fair is foul and foul is fair; and when Macbeth asks: "What is the night?" Lady Macbeth answers: "Almost at odds with morning, which is which." Meaning is lost in equivocation; it is extended and distorted until it means the contrary; and in Macbeth's single state of man

> nothing is
> But what is not.

What is and what is not are confounded until thought sickens; meaning and being are destroyed. At the appearance of Banquo's Ghost, Lady Macbeth tells her husband that he looks only on a stool. But she is wrong; it is her tragedy to see no more than a stool, and at the end of Macbeth's life it is his tragedy to see nothing, and to say that life is a tale signifying nothing. He would trammel up the consequence of what he does; he would act without relation to the world. But no human action is without consequence: it extends before and after to involve character in every aspect of the world, and human life is a tale signifying everything. At the end Macbeth can say only that his wife should have died hereafter; he can feel not even the urgent and personal meaning of death. He has no announcement to make of who he is; he has no identity left with which to cheer himself up. He has words only to record his despair, that life is a poor player, and that he has lived long enough.

Character cannot exist apart from the natural arrangement. In "thynges subiecte to Nature," Sir Thomas Elyot wrote in *The Governor*, "nothynge of hym selfe onely may be norisshed; but whan he hath distroyed that where with he dothe participate by the ordre of his creation, he hym selfe of necessitie muste than perisshe, wherof ensuethe universall dissolution." The perception that evil is a loss of being and of meaning is central to the Christian tradition. Evil has no existence; it is an absence of what ought to exist, and the wish of the

Enemy is that we should think he exists, for by thinking so we give evil existence and sanctuary in our own person. The perception that evil is a negation is figured in the stories of Othello and Timon and Coriolanus and Macbeth. In the encounter with their own characters, they are unable to arrive at a resolution, and are divided from their being. Their personalities are emptied; they suffer the inroads of nothingness and irrationality into the mind and will, and the invasion of whatever terrible vacancy it is that dispossesses the spirit.

VII

These three Mediterranean tragedies are the bleakest points of Shakespeare's vision. The greatness of his vision is variety and a largeness of possibility; but in *Othello, Timon of Athens,* and *Coriolanus* there is instead a restriction of the vision to character defeated by itself, and in this atmosphere of confinement and calculation we are moved only by individual horrors. In *Macbeth,* on the other hand, our thoughts are directed both to what Macbeth does and to a larger action. There is in *Macbeth* the continuous religious awareness that belongs to Shakespeare's northern tragedies. Both the worlds, nature and heaven, move against their desperate offender; nature replies with storm and darkness, and Macbeth's opponents have the help of heaven. "In the great hand of God I stand," Banquo says, and Macduff goes to England to pray for aid "with Him above" to "ratify the work." God deals between Macduff and Malcolm, and there is no equivocation in heaven:

> Angels are bright still, though the brightest fell.
> Though all things foul would wear the brows of grace,
> Yet grace must look so still.

Heaven is a witness, and it takes a part:

> the pow'rs above
> Put on their instruments.

The religious judgments of *Macbeth* are never in uncertainty. We are told of Christian history from the fall of the angels to Golgotha to the crack of doom, and Scotland is ransomed by an army of God's soldiers; like Helena and the Duke in *All's Well* and *Measure for Measure,* Malcolm and his army are the earthly agents of a heavenly effect. Macbeth divides himself from the world and its meaning; he suffers a greater loss than any other of Shakespeare's tragic figures; but in his world there is a correspondingly greater sense of a continuance of meaning that cannot be altered by Macbeth's personal ruin. There is a consciousness, as there is in the histories and comedies, of a pattern working itself out toward an inevitable resolution. The settlement is made not by the protagonist, but by society, by Malcolm and his army, and nothing can prevent the march of society toward peace. The three Mediterranean tragedies are too limited to represent the full scope of Shakespeare's exploration of character and the world; and Shakespeare's vision in *Macbeth* is too clear and assured to ask how we are to be saved. There is no doubt in *Macbeth* about the way to be saved and the way to be damned; the vision, in a new and more profound manner, is of an ordered society; and soon after *Macbeth* Shakespeare wrote *Antony and Cleopatra* and the four romances.

IV

TRAGEDY AND NATURAL FACT

It is at the height of Shakespeare's vision, in *Hamlet* and *King Lear,* that the comparison must be drawn between Shakespeare's vision of nature and Bacon's and Spenser's. The histories and comedies share Bacon's and Spenser's effort toward certainty; *Othello* and *Macbeth* record the defeat of every effort of character. But in *Hamlet* and *King Lear* we witness the encounter between character and both aspects of nature, things and the meaning of things, the province of Bacon's philosophy and of Spenser's. There is no constriction of the imaginative atmosphere in *Hamlet* and *King Lear;* there is instead, in Sir Thomas Elyot's phrase, a universal dissolution, and a constant crossing of things with their meaning. The damned souls of *Hamlet* and *King Lear,* Claudius and Edmund and Goneril and Regan and Cornwall, are not the protagonists; and what happens at the end to Hamlet and Lear cannot be called defeat. There are too many other possibilities; further meanings crowd upon the events; there is a continuous consciousness both of persons and events in themselves and of what they signify, and it is this double awareness of change and of what is beyond change that suggests a comparison between Bacon's exploration of things in themselves, Spenser's vision of a religious continuance beyond things, and Shakespeare's endeavor of the imagination.

II

Bacon's plan was to know and take part in the world of things as they are; and in *Hamlet* and *King Lear* Shakespeare investigates what it means to know and take part in the world. Othello and Macbeth divide themselves from the world, but Hamlet and Lear are compelled to search into themselves and their natural situation and to decide upon action and belief. In what Hamlet and Lear do and suffer and know, Shakespeare investigates what it means, not to forfeit ourselves, but to be ourselves, to follow natural feeling, and to share in natural life: what it means to belong to the world, and to be addressed by the countless loyalties that draw us into the world.

The immediate subject of *Hamlet* and *King Lear* is the natural bond between father and child. This is what first engages our feelings; Hamlet is important because he is a son, and Lear because he is a father. Perhaps this natural relation was a particular preoccupation of Shakespeare's imagination; we think of Prince Hal and Falstaff together, but they act out the relation between Prince Hal and his father, and we think of Miranda, not with Ferdinand, but as she sits at the feet of Prospero. "If there be any truly-naturall law," Montaigne wrote, "that is to say, any instinct, universally and perpetually imprinted," then next to the law of self-preservation is "the affection which the engenderer beareth his off-spring." There are moving appeals made to this natural allegiance at the beginning of *Hamlet* and *King Lear*; they are appeals that set in motion the tragic plot, and at the end their importance surpasses the necessity of self-preservation. The Ghost addresses Hamlet to demand revenge in the name of natural feeling:

> If thou hast nature in thee, bear it not.

And at the division of the kingdom Lear appeals to natural feeling in his daughters:

> Which of you shall we say doth love us most?
> That we our largest bounty may extend
> Where nature doth with merit challenge?

These are appeals to what is deep in human affections, the "manifold and strong" bond by which the child is joined to the father. Hamlet will wipe away all other records from his memory; and though Lear and Gloucester are foolish old men, and though their lives are nearly over, they find it suddenly important, as they approach the moment at which natural life will be taken from them, to discover and assure themselves of their children's natural love. They would, as Gloucester says, unstate themselves to be in a due resolution. Their progress toward resolution occupies the remainder of their lives; and what life is left to Hamlet is a similar progress toward resolution, and toward resolve.

These are the immediate subjects of Shakespeare's imagination. And they are large enough. But they are enlarged by further issues: Hamlet and Lear are driven to the furthest limits of their natural situation, and the question becomes what it means to participate in the world and to play the part of a son or a father. Regan says to Lear that natural life in him stands on "the very verge" of its confine. The events of *Hamlet* and *King Lear* represent the very verge of natural existence; it is this extremity of the tragic vision that, as Charles Lamb said, defies acting, and it is here that the question raised by the tragic vision, what we shall do to be saved, is seen in its full significance. There is great importance in what Hamlet does and what Lear believes; and there is more than this; in the history of Western thought, *Hamlet* and *King Lear* are our most extensive poetic exploration of the consequence of acting and believing. The problem before

Hamlet is how to act the part of a son whose father has been murdered; it is stretched to the limit of what it means to do any act. And in the exploration of belief that Shakespeare undertook in *King Lear*, the faith that Lear has in his daughters becomes a question of whether it is possible to hold any natural belief, until in the storm, in the breakdown of every natural arrangement, Lear encounters in the person of Poor Tom what seems to be "the thing itself."

Bacon's great plan was to turn our attention to the first aspect of nature, things in themselves and their natural causes. *Hamlet* and *King Lear* are Shakespeare's exploration of natural causes; and they ask the question of what it means to perform this exploration, whether the consequence is good or ill. When Lear asks the cause of thunder, it is as if Bacon's plan were being carried out; and there is a deeper question raised when Lear asks if there is a "cause in nature that makes these hard hearts." Bacon's plan of action and belief was to know the world and share in it, shaping it according to the dream of human power. *Hamlet* and *King Lear* were not written in reply; yet they are Shakespeare's exploration of the consequence of knowing and sharing in natural life. The Mediterranean tragedies are understandable in natural terms and accept the limits of natural knowledge; the causes of acting and believing are within natural character. In *Hamlet* and *King Lear* natural character is in doubt, and natural understanding is tested at the farthest extreme of natural existence. At these most distant reaches of Shakespeare's tragic journey, the question of how we are to be saved is a question of whether a natural philosophy is sufficient to be the core of a view of life, whether things in themselves can be explained by natural causes, and what the consequence is to the human spirit of being compelled to ask this question.

III

Hamlet confronts his father's death; the fact of his world is that a father is dead. And he does nothing. He delays; and there has been much throwing about of brains in this matter. There are those who find excuses for his delay, and those who blame him; some blame Shakespeare, and others, condemning the author of the lost Hamlet play for providing Shakespeare with intractable material, stab through the arras of the First Quarto and kill Thomas Kyd. It is suggested by a few that Hamlet does not in truth delay, that he only seems to, and that we are wrong to think he does. But surely Hamlet's delay is a fact, and perhaps the essential fact, of his encounter with his father's death. The play itself is a delaying action: it does not march toward a moment of finality, but is a constant evasion of finality; it moves backward, like a crab, while Hamlet discovers what has happened before the play began. His progress is an advance in recognition; he tells the Players that they hold the mirror up to nature, and before the court he presents a play that catches the conscience of the King; before his mother he holds up a glass where she may see her inmost part, and when he is alone he makes known himself. His advance in knowledge is attended by a hectic energy and by wild and whirling words; some deep-seated fear is represented in his delay. There is uncertainty in not knowing; but there is a dread of knowing, and in his antic disposition and his thrusting away of Ophelia there is figured the cruelty and suffering that spring from this fear of what it means to be a son whose father is dead.

Hamlet's mind is filled with the consciousness that demands are made upon him by his father's death; there is some rôle that he must take in the world; something must be done; and when the Ghost makes known its murder, Hamlet cries: "O my prophetic soul!" But he holds back from playing the part of a son; he stands irresolute, his mind at war, like Isabella's, between will and will not. Even in his sorrow there are contradictions. His grief, Claudius says, is sweet and commendable in his "nature," and in Claudius himself "nature" fights with "discretion." But it is against nature, Claudius says, to mourn unreasonably:

> Fie! 'tis a fault to heaven,
> A fault against the dead, a fault to nature,
> To reason most absurd, whose common theme
> Is death of fathers, and who still hath cried,
> From the first corse till he that died to-day,
> "This must be so."

The death of fathers, Gertrude says, belongs to the natural plan:

> Thou know'st 'tis common. All that lives must die,
> Passing through nature to eternity.
>
> Ay, madam, it is common.
>   If it be,
> Why seems it so particular with thee?

Natural feeling demands that we mourn the death of a father, but the natural arrangement of the world requires that we accept it. We must accept the world as it is in fact, and consent to things as they are; it is necessary to share in natural life. Hamlet holds back from this necessity. We know, Hamlet's mother says, that it is a necessity common to our natural history; but it is particular with Hamlet.

Hamlet is addressed by his situation. But its demands are contradictory, and there is uncertainty in Denmark about whether natural feeling is to be obeyed. Polonius says of Hamlet and his mother that "nature makes them partial," and Hamlet, his sword drawn, remembers natural affection:

> Soft! now to my mother!
> O heart, lose not thy nature; let not ever

TRAGEDY AND NATURAL FACT

> The soul of Nero enter this firm bosom.
> Let me be cruel, not unnatural.

In Laertes natural grief fights with shame:

> nature her custom holds,
> Let shame say what it will.

Laertes accepts natural feeling as a cue for action:

> I am satisfied in nature,
> Whose motive in this case should stir me most
> To my revenge.

But Hamlet holds back from taking his place in the arrangement of natural feeling; and while Hamlet is wrong to delay, Laertes is wrong not to delay. The claims of natural feeling are ambiguous; things in themselves are associated with evils that make the validity of natural loyalties uncertain. There are things rank and gross in the natural world:

> Fie on't! ah, fie! 'Tis an unweeded garden
> That grows to seed; things rank and gross in nature
> Possess it merely.

It happens in particular men that they have

> some vicious mole of nature in them,
> As in their birth, — wherein they are not guilty,
> Since nature cannot choose his origin.

They carry

> the stamp of one defect,
> Being nature's livery, or fortune's star.

The stamp of natural imperfection is on Hamlet's mother:

> For use almost can change the stamp of nature,
> And either master the devil or throw him out.

His uncle is a canker of nature:

> And is't not to be damn'd
> To let this canker of our nature come
> In further evil?

There is doubt, as there is in the problem plays, of whether it is well to follow natural feeling and to be ourselves. Helena knows "all the miseries which nature owes," and Hamlet knows

> The heartache, and the thousand natural shocks
> That flesh is heir to.

The First and Second Lords in *All's Well* are horrified at what things we are as we are ourselves; Isabella asks Angelo how he would be if God should judge him as he is; and Hamlet asks Polonius:

> Use every man after his desert, and who should scape whipping?

Human nature is frail and guilty; the Queen sees black and grained spots in her very soul, and virtue, Hamlet says, cannot so inoculate our old stock but we shall relish of it. Polonius says that his son may be accused, without dishonor, of gaming, drinking, fencing, swearing, quarreling, and drabbing — they are the stamp of nature, the "taints of liberty." They are common; they are the frailty of unredeemed nature, like Bertram's natural rebellion:

> A savageness in unreclaimed blood,
> Of general assault.

Human life, a lord says in *All's Well*, is of a mingled yarn, good and ill together. Nature binds us to mourn the death of a father, but at the same time nature makes us heir to shocks, afflictions, and whipping. Nature is defective, it has somehow been damaged, there are weeds and cankers in it, and a quality rank and gross.

IV

The contradictions of Hamlet's natural situation are given form at the address of the Ghost. The Ghost makes known its "foul and most unnatural murther," the act "most foul, strange, and unnatural." Poison was poured through the "natural gates and alleys" of its body, and because of this deed all Denmark is infected. The address of the Ghost is a further step in Hamlet's knowledge; through the Ghost, the events of the past are made articulate. And in making known the past, the Ghost lays claim on the present. What is made known becomes a command: Hamlet is required to give more than sorrow or consent; he is commanded to act, to play his rôle, to commit himself, to attack his world and set it right. On a cold parapet in a sick country, above the sounds of a drunken wassail, the Ghost appeals to what is natural in Hamlet: "If thou hast nature in thee, bear it not." Hamlet's reply can hardly be so simple and so unequivocal as Ophelia's response to the bidding of a more worldly father: "I shall obey, my lord."

The Ghost appeals to natural feeling, the bond that draws parent and child together; it is "thou poor ghost," and the figure of a father. It is an honest ghost; Hamlet will take its word for a thousand pound. Yet its command, delivered in the name of nature, is that a murder which was most foul, strange, and unnatural be revenged by acts which will be, as Horatio says at the end, "carnal, bloody, and unnatural." The command of the Ghost is to repeat the violence of the past; Hamlet is enjoined to prolong a history of natural pain. The Ghost is not only the figure of a father; it is a shape of terror, and a recollection of the guilt of all natural action:

> I am thy father's spirit,
> Doom'd for a certain term to walk the night,
> And for the day confin'd to fast in fires,

> Till the foul crimes done in my days of nature
> Are burnt and purg'd away.

It is a figure murdered in the state of its natural imperfection, an emblem of the contradictory loyalties and horrors of the natural condition: a spirit and a father, shocking and pitiable, a figure whose history is a summary of the fond affections and foul crimes done in our days of nature. The Ghost is a representation of what it means to share in natural life; and its command is that Hamlet too must participate in the contradictions of natural feeling, and take his place in the common natural history.

The Ghost is a shape from beyond natural life that invades Hamlet's natural situation. It is a piece of the past that cannot rest, that returns to the present, wandering in pain between the lands of the dead and the living. Its address is the interruption of a voice from outside the condition of nature, which shakes us with thoughts beyond our natural reason:

> Making night hideous, and we fools of nature
> So horridly to shake our disposition
> With thoughts beyond the reaches of our souls.

We are "fools of nature," and the story of the prison house beyond the prison of Denmark would harrow us with fear and wonder; our natural character is shaken by touches of eternity. And Hamlet cannot reject this voice from a continuance beyond things in themselves; he must admit into his natural existence an uninvited and outrageous intruder. In Hamlet's perplexity he is addressed not only by the ambiguous demands of natural feeling but by claims from an undiscovered country that puzzle the will. The Ghost is a shape that draws men into madness; it leads Hamlet to the extremity of his natural situation, the point at which the necessity to act and the fear of acting are made acute. Our days of nature, the condition of life, are haunted by demands from the condition of death; images of death fill Hamlet's mind, and there is seen to be an equation between acting and dying.

In comedy, to share in nature is to accept a design moving toward a happy ending; only the fools and the dissenters, Bottom or Jaques or Falstaff, daff the world aside and bid it pass. Hamlet is the tragic dissenter, holding himself apart from the world; he is commanded by natural feeling to act, but his mind is divided by his consciousness of the meanings that surround natural action. He will not accept the common theme of nature, the death of fathers; he recoils from the frailty of women; he puts on an antic disposition; and when he acts, he stabs through a curtain. He thinks of suicide, the ultimate dissent from the world and refusal to take part in it; the question, as he puts it to himself, is more than a matter of acting or delaying: it is to be or not to be, to live or die to the world, to share in the world or to abstain, to stand aside, to end the heartache and the thousand natural shocks.

He asks bitterly who calls him coward; and certainly there is figured in his anguish and delay a profound fear of the consequence of taking arms in the world. To know the world as Hamlet is brought to know it is to discover that the motive and cue for action is never sufficient. The elder Hamlet and the elder Fortinbras acted with a heroic simplicity; they belonged to a past in which action was simple and clear, and kingdoms were gaged and forfeited by single combat. Yet their motive was no more than "a most emulate pride," and now in the army of the younger Fortinbras twenty thousand men go to their graves like beds for "a fantasy and trick of fame." This is action, and it stings Hamlet's conscience; yet the twenty thousand men fight for a plot not wide enough to hide the slain, "for an eggshell." There is no great argument for action; to act is greatly to find quarrel in a straw. The First Player weeps for Hecuba; this is acting; but it is acting that a man might play, done "all for nothing," and in "a dream of passion." Hamlet knows it well; he himself acts madness, and could have a fellowship in a cry of players. In Denmark there is too much acting or too little; it has lost the name of action, and has become, for Hamlet, suffering. There are aspects of Hamlet's natural situation through which we arrive at the furthest limits of what it means to act; the Ghost is a voice from the deepest cellarage of the mind, and in Hamlet's antic disposition there are phrases and accents that seem more than pretending.

For the consequence, both of acting and of not acting, is fatal; it is a choice, like Coriolanus', that cannot be resolved. To delay, to refrain from sharing in the world, is to surrender life; but to participate in natural life is another kind of suicide. There is the death of non-commitment and the death of commitment. At the beginning Hamlet confronts his father's death; at the end, when there is in his heart such a kind of gaingiving as would perhaps trouble a woman, we know that he confronts his own. To share in the tragic world is to engage ourselves to a design drawing us toward death; the command of the Ghost is that Hamlet participate in the natural arrangement of death, the demand that the dead generation makes upon the living, that they too share in the common mortality. Hamlet's choice is not so much to be or not to be; it is a choice, as the First Gravedigger says, between two ways of dying:

> Here lies the water; good. Here stands the man; good. If the man go to this water and drown himself, it is, will he nill he, he goes — mark you that. But if the water come to him and drown him, he drowns not himself.

In the encounter between character and the world, to act is to know the world and go to meet it. For here, the Gravedigger says, lies the point: "if I drown myself wittingly, it argues an act." Either way is drowning; to act is to die knowingly.

V

The necessity of sharing in the world is figured in the address of the Ghost. Yet the fear that attaches to the Ghost suggests the consequence of sharing in the world; in Hamlet's delay is represented the unwillingness of the mind to surrender itself to the persons and events of the world, and the longing of the mind to be engaged to what is certain and absolute and beyond the reach of time. We desire to give ourselves not to things but to what is beyond things, the perfect image; there is a dread of belonging to the world. When Macbeth prepares to do the deed that shakes his thought, he fears the deed less than the consequence. No act is the be-all and the end-all; at the root of great tragedy, as Mr. Arthur Sewell says, is the idea that any act involves us in the evil of time. There is a fear deeply grounded in the human condition that the consequences of what we do stretch out in time and involve us in the pattern of time: that no act is completed, but becomes a part of the continuing action of our lives. The dream of childhood, and of comedy, is that we are outside time, that we shall never grow up, and that there are no clocks in the forest; at the moment when we know and confess ourselves to be within time, we admit death into our person. The involvement in time and death is represented by Christianity in the story of the Fall and the loss of Eden; and the fear of this involvement is what ultimately moves us in *Hamlet*. When Hamlet waits with Horatio before the fencing match, it is known to Hamlet and to us that whatever he does will be a consent to time and death, and a step into the dark; when he acts it will be "rashly," and "prais'd be rashness for it."

VI

I have taken *Hamlet* to be a play about acting within the natural situation; I should like to consider *King Lear* as a play about believing. And at first it seems possible to speak of *King Lear* with more assurance. In *Hamlet* meanings are suggested to us; the events seem perplexed with meanings just beyond our grasp, and our minds are shaken with thoughts beyond our reach. What strikes us in *King Lear* is the uncompromising clarity of right and wrong; there are no shadows; good and evil are in open encounter, and there is no uncertainty about which is which. We are able, up to a point, to state the issues of the play with confidence. But when we have reached that point we find these certainties to have been misleading: the clarity of right and wrong is a preliminary to a larger issue, an issue in which character and event, because they are simpler and more distinct, are more formidable; an issue, that is, of belief.

The problem confronting Lear and Gloucester and Albany and Edgar is not how to act within their world, but how they are to explain it, whether they can find something in their world to believe in, whether, indeed, a world of intolerable natural distress can be believed in. Action is not required of them; it is the enemy, Edmund and Goneril and Regan and Cornwall, who act, and until the end they act quickly and well. Lear performs one deed, the division of the kingdom, and it is an action whose terrible consequences occupy the play. The burden of Lear is to suffer, and to suffer "most i' th' mind." He believes in nature; and the question is whether he can preserve his belief in the face of unnaturalness. Mr. John F. Danby distinguishes between those in the play who believe in a "benignant nature," and those who attach their belief or their fortunes to a "malignant nature." Certainly there is a difference between what Edmund means by "nature," and what Cordelia means; but from another point of view *King Lear* is a play in which everyone believes, and announces his belief, in some kind of nature. The setting is pre-Christian; we have a society in which belief can never, as it were, be more than preliminary, but it is a society reaching toward belief, and this effort toward faith is figured in the suffering of Lear in the storm and his discovery in Poor Tom of "the thing itself."

It would seem that Shakespeare changed the setting to suit his purposes. *The True Chronicle History of King Leir* is firmly Christian; there is a storm, but it is the point at which Leir's belief in the Christian God is confirmed, not lost. At a stroke of thunder the Messenger sent to murder him quakes and lets fall the dagger, and there is no need to ask the cause of thunder; the heavens have sent down to take Leir's part. Leir and Cordella are reunited, their enemies are vanquished, and Leir thanks heaven, for "God protected him from all their spite." The laws of nature in *King Leir* are strong and sacred, and above them are the laws of God, that are never in doubt and that no event can harm. Clearly Shakespeare's purposes were otherwise; and in this matter he followed opposite artistic procedures in *Hamlet* and *King Lear*. The old story of Amleth took place before the introduction of Christianity into Denmark; either Shakespeare or the author of the lost Hamlet play is responsible for its introduction into Shakespeare's play. In *King Lear* the Christian setting of the source is excluded. A play about revenge is perplexed by the inclusion of Christian feeling, and a play about belief is complicated by its absence. It would seem to have been Shakespeare's intention to complicate and perplex, and to explore the validity of a natural philosophy; and in *King Lear* his purpose seems to have been to investigate, in the storm and the discovery of the thing itself, an unaided belief in nature alone, and what it means "to know Nature and to follow her."

VII

Orthodox Elizabethan opinion is clear enough about this kind of natural belief. Cecropia, in Sidney's *Arcadia,* believes that natural things are obedient only to themselves: "all things," she says, "follow but the course of their own nature, saving only Man, who while by the pregnancie of his imagination he strives to things supernaturall, meane-while he looseth his owne naturall felicitie." She is an atheist; and Pamela, her cheeks angry red, cries: "Peace (wicked woman) peace." It is not Nature, but God, who orders the things of the world; and God is "a right heavenly Nature indeed, as it were unnaturing them." In *The Atheist's Tragedy,* D'Amville believes that there is nothing in a man beyond what is natural. D'Amville is a villain, and he learns his mortal error: that the Goddess Nature alone is a "foole," and that there is a power above her and above "naturall understanding." The incompleteness of natural understanding and of things in themselves is an argument of Lambert Daneau's in his treatise *The Wonderful Workmanship of the World.* It is an argument contrary to the undertaking that Bacon proposed: the mistake of natural philosophers, Daneau says, is to confine their study to "thinges themselves," to "certein lowe and meane degrees, and an uncertein force, whiche is respected after their Creation, and whiche thei terme Nature." These natural philosophers "make the cause of the thyng, of that whiche thei call the thyng it selfe," and "verie many of those Natural Philosophers, dooe at the length beecome indeede, verie naturalles, that is too saie, fleshely men, and Atheistes, not knowyng, or regardyng God." According to Christian doctrine, things in themselves are created and sustained by the religious order, and to believe that the cause of a thing is the thing itself is to deny God. Nature is no more than God's instrument, an ax, as Hooker said, in the hand of the carpenter.

This is the Christian estimate of natural belief; and it is plain in *King Lear* that Edmund is a naturalist. He is a "verie naturalle," and in a Christian context he would be an atheist; some of his words are used later by the atheist D'Amville. Edmund believes in the law of his own nature; he would be himself alone, putting his trust, like Parolles, in simply the thing he is. He repudiates natural feeling, the arrangement of the family, the natural bond of love, and the "idle and fond bondage" of an aged father. He rejects all natural demands except the obligation of self-fulfillment, a natural law that moves in lusty stealth, that is the enemy of law, and a principle not of justice or order or love but of personal *virtù*, proposing to those who listen that one part of the natural world, their own natures, can grow and prosper alone. Edmund is wrong; and at the end of his life he seems to know that he was wrong:

> Some good I mean to do,
> Despite of mine own nature.

As he lies dying, bound upon the wheel he thought he could turn, he seems to confess that his nature cannot exist independently of the moral arrangement of the world.

Yet Lear has our concern and sympathy when he puts his trust in what is natural in his daughters and himself, and when he confronts what natural philosophy calls "the thynge it self." His belief in nature is of a different sort, that commands our pity and respect, and the question in our minds is whether his belief can endure. He is like a child, as Goneril and Regan remind him; he asks for things from the world. Yet for this reason he becomes a figure of great and tragic presence: Hamlet is addressed by his situation, it speaks to him, but Lear makes his own address to the world and his own demands of it. He asks for Regan's natural tenderness:

> Thy tender-hefted nature shall not give
> Thee o'er to harshness;

and for her recognition of natural duty:

> Thou better know'st

> The offices of nature, bond of childhood,
> Effects of courtesy, dues of gratitude.

He calls on the natural powers to witness his disowning of Cordelia:

> For, by the sacred radiance of the sun,
> The mysteries of Hecate and the night;
> By all the operation of the orbs
> From whom we do exist and cease to be;
> Here I disclaim all my paternal care.

He would have the Goddess Nature curse Goneril:

> Hear, Nature, hear! dear goddess, hear!
> Suspend thy purpose, if thou didst intend
> To make this creature fruitful.

He summons the elements to attack her:

> You nimble lightnings, dart your blinding flames
> Into her scornful eyes! Infect her beauty,
> You fen-suck'd fogs, drawn by the pow'rful sun,
> To fall and blast her pride!

Gloucester, surrounded and blinded by his enemies, calls on his son for what the Ghost asks of Hamlet, revenge in the name of nature:

> Edmund, enkindle all the sparks of nature
> To quit this horrid act.

And in the storm Lear calls on "the stor'd vengeances of heaven." In a situation of natural suffering grown intolerable, he demands from the nature of things a wild natural justice:

> Blow, winds, and crack your cheeks! rage! blow!
> You cataracts and hurricanoes, spout
> Till you have drench'd our steeples, drown'd the cocks!
> You sulph'rous and thought-executing fires,
> Vaunt-couriers to oak-cleaving thunderbolts,
> Singe my white head! And thou, all-shaking thunder,

> Strike flat the thick rotundity o' th' world,
> Crack Nature's moulds, all germens spill at once,
> That make ingrateful man!

The Ghost asks Hamlet, if he has natural feeling in him, for revenge; Lear asks for vengeance from the world, and demands that nature itself be natural. Lear and the nature of things are the mighty opposites; they address each other, and the reply that the world makes is painfully clear.

Two of Lear's daughters answer falsely, and the answer of the third, Cordelia, seems false. She replies in terms of the natural bond:

> I love your Majesty
> According to my bond; no more nor less.

She shows, perhaps, a tardiness in nature, but what she says is a promise, like the promise of Holinshed's Cordeilla, "that I have loved you ever, and will continuallie (while I live) love you as my naturall father." After the storm she returns to fulfill her natural obligation; not all the bonds have been broken. She is still herself; she is queen over her passion; and what she does is a reaffirmation of kindness and the natural relation of father and child, of "love, dear love, and our ag'd father's right." Yet at the division of the kingdom her answer seems to Lear to be "Nothing." When Goneril takes Regan by the hand, he has lost two more daughters. His hundred knights are reduced to fifty to twenty-five to ten to five to nothing: "What need one?" There is division between Cornwall and Albany, and an army from France has entered the scattered kingdom. Unnaturalness is rising around Lear like the wind, and Gloucester in dismay watches the progressive deterioration of every natural pattern:

> These late eclipses in the sun and moon portend no good to us. Though the wisdom of nature can reason it thus and thus, yet nature finds itself scourg'd by the sequent effects. Love cools,

friendship falls off, brothers divide. In cities, mutinies; in countries, discord; in palaces, treason; and the bond crack'd 'twixt son and father. This villain of mine comes under the prediction; there's son against father: the King falls from bias of nature; there's father against child.

The heavens, society, the family, and the self exist in a union of natural interrelation; in spite of natural philosophy — the "wisdom of nature," which reasons, like Edmund, that events in one part of the natural world can take place without regard to the rest of the world — there cannot be division in one natural area without division in the others; all nature feels the wound. Cordelia seems a wretch whom "nature is asham'd" to acknowledge; her offence appears "of such unnatural degree" that it is monstrous. Edgar seems an "Unnatural, detested, brutish villain! worse than brutish!" Lear and Gloucester are mistaken; truth and seeming, as in Denmark, are not the same; but unnatural events are taking place that are real enough. In Oswald "nature disclaims," Goneril and Regan are "unnatural hags," Gloucester likes not their "unnatural dealing," and Edmund piously responds: "Most savage and unnatural!" There is, as Edmund says, "unnaturalness between the child and the parent."

The division of the kingdom sets the tragic plot in motion, and it is followed by division between king and subject, father and child, and brother and brother, until in the storm there is division throughout the natural world. Sir Thomas Elyot wrote that the "moste damnable vice and moste agayne iustice, in myne oppinion, is ingratitude, commenly called unkyndnesse." Ungrateful men are "moche wars than beestes." It is this unkindness that spreads through *King Lear* like the poison through Denmark. Ingratitude is doubly unkind: it breaks the bond between parent and child, and its personal consequence is a distortion of kind itself, a reduction of human character to the level of the animals. Lear dreads that he will forget his "nature" and go mad; for what he took to be Cordelia's ingratitude,

> like an engine, wrench'd my frame of nature
> From the fix'd place.

Goneril's ingratitude ties "Sharp-tooth'd unkindness, like a vulture," to Lear's heart. He will be a comrade with the wolf and owl, and Edgar will disguise himself in

> the basest and most poorest shape
> That ever penury, in contempt of man,
> Brought near to beast.

Seeing him, Lear thinks that

> nothing could have subdu'd nature
> To such a lowness but his unkind daughters.

Ingratitude is an unkindness that destroys character and identity; it wrenches the self from the fixed place; it is a "contempt of man." There has been, as one of Lear's knights says, a great abatement of kindness. In the storm Lear holds another trial of his daughters' hearts, and what he asks now is:

> Then let them anatomize Regan. See what breeds about her heart. Is there any cause in nature that makes these hard hearts?

In the storm it seems that the cause of thunder is nature itself; that at the center of human nature there is unkindness; that it is through our own natures, as Edmund jubilantly announces, that we are all that we are evil in; and that only in despite of ourselves do we do some good. Lear will not tax the elements with unkindness; yet they are servile ministers to join with two pernicious daughters; and Gloucester in his blindness has nowhere to turn but to the kind gods.

VIII

In the comedies, and in the tragedies of the southern world, it is enough for character to be itself; in ourselves we have a natural goodness and a natural nobility. It would have been enough for Othello and Timon and Coriolanus to have remained themselves, and to have preserved their natural balance of reason and passion; and in Antony's good night to Brutus, it is praise enough that Brutus' life was gentle and the elements so mixed in him that the Goddess Nature might say to all the world that Brutus was a man. But in the problem plays, and in *Hamlet* and *King Lear*, there is doubt whether it is sufficient to be our natural selves. Horatio is a man who is not passion's slave, and in whom blood and judgment are well commingled; he is Othello without Othello's weaknesses; and Hamlet will wear him in his heart of hearts. Yet to be Horatio is not to be the hero of the story; greater demands are made of Hamlet than are dreamt of in Horatio's natural philosophy. And in *King Lear* it is Edmund, the villain, who would be sufficient in himself. The question is whether natural causes are enough to explain and save ourselves — whether, more simply, it is enough to be a man.

Lear has ever slenderly known himself. But he asks questions; he asks which of his daughters loves him most, and he asks other questions that begin an exploration of himself. "Who am I, sir?" he asks Oswald, and to Goneril he says: "Are you our daughter?" He asks those around him: "Doth any here know me?" He asks the question that Oedipus puts to those at Thebes: "Who is it that can tell me who I am?" There are similarities between the stories of Oedipus and Lear. They are two old and angry kings divided from their kingdoms; Creon and Edmund follow the law of *physis*; unnatural children quarrel for the throne; and two faithful daughters bring restoration. And there is a similarity in what Oedipus and Lear discover about themselves. They inquire into their identity, into what Pamela in the *Arcadia* calls the darkest of all natural secrets, the heart of man. Their inquiry is forced upon them, and becomes, like Hamlet's delay, a part of their suffering. They are divided from what clothes and protects them, and their discovery of who they are is a moment of dread, like Kurtz' discovery at the heart of darkness: "The horror! the horror!" It is a moment when Oedipus cries out at the wandering of his thought; and Lear, coming upon the figure of Poor Tom, tears at his raiment and asks:

Is man no more than this? Consider him well. Thou ow'st the worm no silk, the beast no hide, the sheep no wool, the cat no perfume. Ha! Here's three on's are sophisticated! Thou art the thing itself; unaccommodated man is no more but such a poor, bare, forked animal as thou art.

He has, it seems, found essential human nature, from which no further superfluity can be divided; he has discovered the thing itself.

It is as if Bacon's plan had been completed to explore things as they are and find out their natural causes. And at this moment the play is closest to what Mr. James calls Shakespeare's bleak and merely exploratory vision. At the crisis of Lear's spiritual progress, his words are close to what Montaigne says in *The Apology of Raymond Sebond*: that "man is the onely forsaken and out-cast creature, naked on the bare earth, fast found and swathed, having nothing to cover and arme himselfe withall but the spoile of others; whereas Nature hath clad and mantled all other creatures, some with shels, some with huskes, with rindes, with haire, with wooll, with stings, with bristles, with hides, with mosse, with feathers, with skales, with fleeces, and with silke." Man is not an animal, he is worse than the animals, and only through vanity does he distinguish himself from them; animals may "as well esteeme us beasts, as we them." Is it possible, Montaigne asks, "to imagine any thing so ridiculous, as this miserable and wreched creature, which is not so much as master of himselfe, exposed and subject to offences of all things, and yet dareth to call himselfe Master and Emperour of this Universe?"

In Book I of *The Faerie Queene*, the figure of Despair sits beside a corpse killed with a rusty knife; he tries to hang himself, as he has tried a thousand times before, and his words to the Red Cross Knight were chosen by Conrad for a motto, that death after life does greatly please. It is despair, Edgar says twice, that we find in Gloucester; he stands on the verge of his imagined cliff to address the kind gods and renounce the natural world:

> O you mighty gods!
> This world I do renounce, and in your sights
> Shake patiently my great affliction off.
> If I could bear it longer and not fall
> To quarrel with your great opposeless wills,
> My snuff and loathed part of nature should
> Burn itself out.

Lear's natural philosophy falls to madness, and Gloucester's to despair. Their natural suffering passes beyond the point at which it can be borne; the storm is too rough for "nature to endure," and natural belief cannot withstand this "unnatural and bemadding sorrow." Life itself is their great affliction. Before and during the storm, nature is wrenched, forgotten, constrained, oppressed, cracked, afflicted, and subdued: after the storm, nature is spoken of only eight times, as if it were no longer an explanation of the events; it seems loathed, abused, ruined, and under a general curse. The sight of Poor Tom made Gloucester think that a man is a worm; and now Gloucester says:

> As flies to wanton boys are we to th' gods.
> They kill us for their sport.

These words are not all that Shakespeare would have us think; yet they are words that we remember.

IX

And there is a worse discovery than the recognition of the thing itself. It is the death of Cordelia, the scene that Dr. Johnson found too painful to reread. She has done her best, in her short life, to arrange a happy ending, but every measure fails her. In death the defenceless and unaccommodated human spirit seems in truth to be no different from the spirit of a bare, forked animal:

> Why should a dog, a horse, a rat, have life,
> And thou no breath at all?

It is the last question that Lear asks of the nature of things; and there is no answer. The death of Cordelia is a concluding horror; it seems almost arbitrary; it is forced upon us. Yet it is a fact of Shakespeare's tragic vision; and it is at this moment that Kent asks: "Is this the promis'd end?"

Greek tragedy does not conclude with death; Orestes does not die at the end of the *Oresteia,* or Oedipus at the end of *Oedipus the King.* It is the Elizabethan tragic world that comes to an end in death, the simplest and most fundamental fact of the Elizabethan tragic vision. Lear announces at the beginning that he will crawl unburdened toward his death, Hamlet thinks of death in his most famous soliloquy, and it is in all our minds when he tells Horatio: "But thou wouldst not think how ill all's here about my heart." As Shakespeare's comic vision moves toward the moment of marriage, Shakespearian tragedy moves toward the moment of dying, the event that gives final shape to the encounter between character and things in themselves.

X

Sir Andrew Aguecheek announces that he is a natural fool. In their suffering, Shakespeare's tragic figures speak likewise:

after the storm Lear calls himself the "natural fool of fortune," and Hamlet, at the approach of the Ghost, calls himself and all men "fools of nature." It is the perception of tragedy that to share in the world is to be the victim of the world; to be what the Duke speaks of when he says to Claudio: "Merely thou art death's fool."

Jaques and Falstaff dissent from the continuance of the comic world; the dissenters of the tragic world are Hamlet and Lear. They are commanded to know and follow nature; there is a necessity to act and believe; but the consequence is death, and something of this contradiction is expressed in the folly and madness of the tragic protagonist. It may be that the comic scenes in *Doctor Faustus* were written by another hand than Marlowe's; but there is something true about their juxtaposition of folly and damnation. Lear and his fool change places; it is the fool who would restore Lear to reason and society. There is no fool in *Hamlet*; Yorick is dead; and it is Hamlet himself who like his ancestor Amleth puts on an antic disposition, and who is driven by some strange and bitter compulsion to speak wild and whirling words. With a "crafty madness," Hamlet "keeps aloof." Like the fool, he is both within and without his situation; it is not only his misfortune, but his tragic privilege, to stand at one remove from the world.

The correspondence between the tragic hero and the fool suggests the peculiar encounter that the tragic hero makes with his world. He is not altogether the world's victim; like the fool, he stands apart. The fool has a strange immortality; he emerges from the jaws of death to announce an epilogue; and the story of the tragic hero includes a similar suggestion that the human spirit both belongs to the world and keeps aloof. Miss Enid Welsford says of the fool: "The serious hero focuses events, forces issues, and causes catastrophes; but the Fool by his mere presence dissolves events, evades issues, and throws doubt on the finality of fact." Hamlet and Lear are serious heroes: they are, perhaps, the most serious of all Shakespeare's heroes. Yet it is Hamlet and Lear who dissolve events, evade issues, and by their mere presence on the stage throw doubt on the finality of fact. Their misfortune and their privilege is to step forward from the world, to know it and judge it, and to play the part of a son or a father.

We must see both Shakespeare and Bacon, Mr. James says, as belonging to the same great movement of the human spirit toward what Bacon called "inclosures of particularity." Certainly Shakespeare's art, like Bacon's natural philosophy, represents an engagement to things in themselves. But it is an engagement that is not made unknowingly in Shakespeare's art. *Hamlet* and *King Lear* are explorations of what it means to know and be committed to things in themselves, and to share, through action and belief, in the course of natural existence; and what Hamlet and Lear discover about the world and themselves is not what Bacon meant when he wrote that "Discoveries carry blessings with them, and confer benefits without causing harm or sorrow to any."

Though Bacon sometimes had in mind his own advancement, his proposal was for the advancing of our knowledge, and he had no doubt that it was well to know: "whatever deserves to exist deserves also to be known, for knowledge is the image of existence." But the discoveries made by Hamlet and Lear are a cause of great harm and sorrow; when Hamlet waits in the hall and Lear will be God's spy, what they do and believe is in spite of what they know. It would be difficult, certainly, to find two temperaments as different as Bacon's and Hamlet's; there is great doubt, in Hamlet's mind, of what it means to know, and knowing, to act. Hamlet also says that knowledge is the image of existence, but he says it with a difference: that there is nothing good or bad but thinking makes it so. Hamlet's increasing understanding is what pains and perplexes him; conscience, he says, makes cowards of us all, and by conscience Hamlet means consciousness itself.

There are two notions about the consequences of knowing, both of ancient standing. The first is that knowledge brings us to certainty and perfect being. But the other, which is associated with Christianity and the vision of great tragedy, is that when knowledge is brought into the world its consequence is sorrow and death. This pain that attaches to knowledge is what Bacon had to defend his enterprise against when he confessed that some men say "that knowledge is of those things which are to be accepted of with great limitation and caution; that the aspiring to over-much knowledge was the original temptation and sin, whereupon ensued the fall of man; that knowledge hath in it somewhat of the serpent." The perception of Sophocles in *Oedipus the King* is that knowledge of ourselves has in it somewhat of the serpent; and in English tragedy this perception is figured in Hamlet's fear and delay, and in Lear's discovery of the thing itself. Bacon proposed knowledge as his great plan of action and belief; in Shakespeare's poetic and dramatic investigation, there are matters that fall beyond Bacon's province. Bacon said that all knowledge was his province, but Shakespeare's vision is concerned with the process of knowing; his subject is the effort toward knowledge, and it is his tragic perception that we act and believe in the face of the pain and death that our knowing implicates us in.

In comedy, death is no more than an episode in the progress of society. The death of Henry IV is part of the natural plan; he has "walk'd the way of nature." But he is succeeded by his son, and his crown is an image of a continuing society. The death of Falstaff, for Mistress Quickly and his comrades, is a moment of sadness and alarm: being down, there are no levers to lift him up, and he dies between twelve and one, at the turning of the tide, fumbling with the sheets and smiling upon his fingers' ends. Yet even Falstaff's death, when Pistol says, "Let us to France," is an event gathered into the tide of English history. It is not so in the tragic world; as the chorus say in *Oedipus at Colonus*, death is the finish. Fortinbras and Edgar will preserve the continuance of society at the end of *Hamlet* and *King Lear*. But this is of no consequence; what happens now is no matter. "It is as natural," Bacon said, "to die as to be born." But this is not the thought in our minds when Hamlet says:

> If thou didst ever hold me in thy heart,
> Absent thee from felicity awhile,
> And in this harsh world draw thy breath in pain,
> To tell my story.

Or Desdemona:

> Farewell.
> Commend me to my kind lord. O, farewell!

Or Lear:

> I know when one is dead, and when one lives.
> She's dead as earth.

Or Macbeth:

> To-morrow, and to-morrow, and to-morrow
> Creeps in this petty pace from day to day
> To the last syllable of recorded time;
> And all our yesterdays have lighted fools
> The way to dusty death.

Or Cleopatra:

> Give me my robe, put on my crown. I have
> Immortal longings in me.

The thought in our minds is that these are the words of human beings who are making what answer they can to the final natural loss, the event that proves the incompleteness of what they have done and believed, of natural philosophy, and of the aspect of nature that is "sensible, mutable, and subject to generation and corruption, respecting all things that have life, and shall have end." The Greek gods were jealous of human mortality, and joined in human battles to share its risks. Death is the fact that makes human life dramatic; it is in the face of death that character announces itself and undertakes the rashness of acting and believing: the moment when we preserve a part of ourselves to make our last address to the world, and when we win a measure of honor through the words by which we report our defeat.

V

TRAGEDY AND "SEEMING"

At the moment of death the secular vision of nature can go no further. There are no more natural causes or natural meanings; the philosophy of things as they are has nothing more to tell us. But it is at this moment that the religious vision turns to the second aspect of nature, a continuance beyond time and death, "spirituall, intelligible and the un-changeable beginning of motion and rest, or rather the vertue, efficient, the preserving cause of all things." Spenser looks toward another stage of certainty, and a time when no more change shall be; the religious argument proposes another way to be saved. There is hope of a different kind of knowledge, that does indeed carry blessings with it. And in *Hamlet* and *King Lear* there are suggestions of this further knowledge: there are hints that the tragic journey may convey the mind toward a manner of understanding that redeems the distress attaching to persons and things. There is something in Hamlet's story more than natural, if philosophy could find it out; the approach of the Ghost, A. C. Bradley says, is "a reminder or a symbol of the connexion of the limited world of ordinary experience with the vaster life of which it is but a partial appearance." So at the end, at Horatio's benediction, "we have an intimation of the same character, and a reminder that the apparent failure of Hamlet's life is not the ultimate truth concerning him." In the histories and comedies we look toward a perfect image of success; in *Othello* and *Macbeth* we witness total defeats. At the end of *Hamlet* and *King Lear* we reach moments that seem beyond success or failure. It seems, at the death of Hamlet and Lear, that nothing is here for tears; the vision passes beyond suffering and natural misfortune, until it is comforting and right that Hamlet will have no more to do with this harsh world, and that Kent should say at the death of Lear: "O, let him pass!" At Colonus, Oedipus prays: "Grant me then, goddesses, passage from life at last." Something of this thought is in our minds at the end of *Hamlet* and *King Lear*; there are phrases and intonations suggesting that all may be well, and that "To die, now," as Oedipus tells his daughters, "would not be so terrible."

II

But these are delicate matters; they are suggestions only of what may be, or what seems to be. It is a modern tendency to find religious symbolism in literature, but there is some doubt of how genuine our interest is in grace, and original sin is fashionable. Certainly religious affairs are in hand in *Measure for Measure* and *All's Well*. It is equally clear, however, that there are plays of Shakespeare's in which our attention is drawn to religious issues hardly at all; questions of this kind do not occupy our minds in the histories and comedies, nor in the tragedies of the Mediterranean world. There are religious suggestions about Hamlet and Cordelia, but there are scarcely any about Othello or Timon or Coriolanus. In Book I of *The Faerie Queene*, Spenser represented holiness in the story of the Red Cross Knight; and in Book II the figure of Sir Guyon stands for natural and classical excellence. Perhaps Hamlet and Othello can be seen in a similar relation as religious and secular protagonists. But this cannot have been Shakespeare's intention; there is no pattern to his plays as there is to the books of *The Faerie Queene*. That Shakespeare was "temperamentally as Christian as Spenser," Mr. W. B. C. Watkins says, "seems beyond dispute." Yet it would seem not to be beyond dispute. For Mr. R. B. Heilman decides that in *King Lear* "we see not only an age that is technically pagan but also a play that is pervaded by Christian influences"; while on the other side Mr. James says: "I am not now concerned to argue, what I think would be extravagant, that there is nowhere in the play implicit Christian feeling; what seems certain is that it was Shakespeare's fully conscious decision not to give to the story any fraction of a Christian context." The matter is in dispute, and this in itself suggests something of the quality of religious possibility in *Hamlet* and *King Lear*.

Yet at the end of Shakespeare's tragic plot there is a movement toward the restoration of what has been lost; and in this concluding movement Shakespeare's vision suggests the third great event of the Christian history of nature, its redemption from time and death. It cannot have been Shakespeare's purpose to suggest this parallel; what we have is the similarity that exists between all great representations of human experience. At the commencement of Shakespeare's tragic plot there is established, as there is in Christian history, the original goodness of nature: Othello, Timon, and Coriolanus have a natural nobility; the Ghost appeals to what is natural in Hamlet, and Lear to what is natural in his daughters; and in Macbeth and Lady Macbeth, as they are by nature, is the milk of human kindness and the compunctious visiting of natural feeling. The tragic plot is set in motion by a fall from this original integrity, and by actions that violate the continuance of nature and society — the alteration of the self, the killing of the king, the division of the kingdom, and the assassination of natural pity. There follows a growing disorder, and nature is scourged by the sequent effects; but at the end there is the hope of a remedy. It is the increasing disorder that forces human life to its extremity; there are great losses, but there is the possibility of a profit that could be reached by no other means than at the boundary of the natural situation.

III

I should like to make a proposal about the Elizabethan revenge play, a proposal that applies, I think, to Hamlet and Cordelia. There are no figures quite like Hamlet and Cordelia in the plays of Marlowe or Webster, but there are figures of this sort in certain Elizabethan revenge plays. Hamlet is a revenger, and to some degree Cordelia is as well; they both bring a measure of restoration to sickened and divided nature. The restorations that they bring about seem sometimes to be almost more than natural; and so it is with other of Shakespeare's characters. Helena and the Duke arrange the happy endings of *All's Well* and *Measure for Measure*, and we are told that what they do is like power divine, or the very hand of heaven, or the showing of a heavenly effect in an earthly actor. The divine Desdemona, if she were able, would restore her kind lord. But she is helpless, and "half asleep" — it is in the three tragedies of the northern world, *Hamlet, King Lear*, and *Macbeth*, that a figure returns from a foreign country and with some success does what he can to set right the tragic world. Hamlet returns from his sea voyage to England; Cordelia returns from France; Malcolm returns to Scotland; and at their reappearance these figures seem more than they were, as if the powers above had put on their instruments.

There are continuous recollections in *Hamlet* of the Christian story. Claudius remembers "the first corse" and "the primal eldest curse," and when the Gravediggers have debated Christian burial and made a joke of Adam's profession, Hamlet remembers Cain and "the first murther." The events of the play are supplemented by religious memories that add depth to the events and suggest their correspondence to recurring events in human history; and the persons of the play, in the doubt and heartsickness of Denmark, appeal to the certainty of heaven. Standing watch in the dead vast and middle of the night, Marcellus thinks of the hallowed time of Christmas; in heaven, Claudius knows, there is no shuffling; there the action lies in its true nature. And these suggestions apply most frequently to Hamlet's act of revenge. It seems that what Hamlet does is the will of heaven:

> For this same lord,
> I do repent; but heaven hath pleas'd it so,
> To punish me with this, and this with me,
> That I must be their scourge and minister.

His revenge seems directed by heaven:

> There's a divinity that shapes our ends,
> Rough-hew them how we will.

Heaven assists him:

> Why, even in that was heaven ordinant.

And at the end, when his revenge is accomplished, he is conveyed by Horatio's farewell into the beauty of grace:

> Good night, sweet prince,
> And flights of angels sing thee to thy rest!

At his death Hamlet is rewarded by words that grant him a level of redemption won by no other of Shakespeare's tragic heroes; a reason is suggested for his revenge and his act of "rashness."

There are puzzling undertones in the Elizabethan revenge plot; there is more in it, I think, than we give it credit for. Revenge is an act of violence; there is a quality of terror

about revenge that is felt even in the two chilling words that
pass between Beatrice and Benedick: "Kill Claudio." One
of Chapman's revengers says reluctantly that he must fall to
doing something, but these are not the sentiments of the
true Elizabethan revenger: John Marston's Antonio expresses
them when he reads from Seneca on the contempt of Fortune
and calls it "Naught els but smoake." The revenger is driven
by a sorrow and desperation beyond Stoic patience, when
"there is so great a fever on goodness," as the Duke says in
Measure for Measure, "that the dissolution of it must cure it."
The act of revenge is not performed in resignation or forti-
tude; it is represented in Hamlet's leap into Ophelia's grave,
or in Antonio's cry, "Let none out-woe me."

At the same time the violence of revenge is associated with
a peculiarly contradictory religious consciousness. In the com-
plexity of their situation, revengers are addressed by both
earth and heaven: "I am torne," one of Tourneur's revengers
says,

> betweene the passion of
> My bloud, and the religion of my soule.

The passionate extremity of their situation drives revengers
to a point at which their actions acquire a more than natural
significance. Antonio and his confederates seem to do heaven's
will:

> thus the hand of heaven chokes
> The throate of murder.

They are congratulated:

> Blest be you all, and may your honours live
> Religiously helde sacred, even for ever and ever.

They will live enclosed in "holy verge of some religious
order," and Chapman's revengers, when their revenge is accomplished, will "forsake the world." The Elizabethan re-

venger ends his life in heaven or a monastery; their deeds are granted an odd religious justification. The religious sanction given Antonio's revenge is far from convincing; it is, indeed, shockingly false; but what is interesting is that Marston felt compelled to attempt it. There is something in the story of revenge that seems to have required, at the cost of manipulating the events, that revenge be placed in a religious framework; and something that made *Hamlet*, as Bradley calls it, the most religious of Shakespeare's tragedies.

The most famous Greek tragedy of revenge, the *Oresteia*, is a story constructed around these two opposites of violence and religious justification. Society in the *Oresteia* is in progress from violence to religious sanctions, and the turning point is Orestes' revenge, an act that is violent and sanctified at once; he kills his mother, but he is defended by Apollo, and at the end the Furies themselves are transfigured. In 1567 the *Oresteia* had a rough but honest Elizabethan descendant, John Pickering's *Horestes*, and, in the intervals between marches and battles and low comedy, *Horestes* is a problem play about the same contradictions in Horestes' revenge. It is an act of public justice that the "law of gods and man doth wil." The "gods," we are told, "have wylled thus," and when Horestes appeals to heaven for guidance, the Vice announces that he is a messenger from the gods to urge Horestes to vengeance. But we are not sure; and to kill his mother is to deny natural feeling:

> Yet lo, dame nature teles me, that I must with willing mind
> Forgive the faute.

The Goddess Nature herself appears on stage to dissuade him:

> Nay, stey, my child, from mothers bloud with draw thy
> bloudy hand.

There is a debate between Horestes and the Goddess Nature;

he rejects her, she goes out lamenting, and the deed is done.
The Vice turns to us and asks:

> And was it not yll
> His mother to kyll?
> I pray you, how saye you?

We have the problem of the contradictory commands of
heaven and earth. The play decides for heaven: Horestes de-
fends himself before an assembly of lords on the ground that
his revenge was the will of the gods; he is crowned with Truth
and Duty and betrothed to Menelaus' daughter; and the play
concludes with a genuinely Aeschylean note, a prayer for the
commonwealth.

These are deep waters; but we are beckoned further by
C. G. Jung and Gilbert Murray. There are stories, Gilbert
Murray says, "deeply implanted in the memory of the race."
There is "something in us which leaps at the sight of them, a
cry of the blood which tells us we have known them always."
One of these is the story of revenge, the story of Hamlet and
Orestes. And there is, I think, a deeper correspondence, between the plot of revenge and Christian history; they share
the same threefold story, the original goodness of nature, its
violation, and the hope of a remedy through the intervention
of a figure whose actions seem more than natural. The Red
Cross Knight is a revenger; he brings redemption to the King
and Queen of Eden; and in Hamlet there is suggested something of the folly and madness and ultimate divinity of those
who suffer and die to set right the world, passing through
nature to eternity. The room of Memory in *The Faerie
Queene* holds records of ancient stories that are never forgotten; and perhaps from some buried memory of the race,
some cellarage of the mind, came this interchange in Marston's *Malcontent*:

> *Orestes*, beware *Orestes*.
> Out beggar.

> I once shall rise,
> Thou rise?
> I at the resurrection.

There is some quality in the revenge plot that involves it in religious matters; there is some liaison between the brutality of revenge and the violence of sanctification. Revenge, Bacon said, is a kind of wild justice; and the chorus in *Agamemnon* cry out that "grace comes somehow violent." Hamlet and Orestes are not religious redeemers; yet there are contradictions about them that approach the paradoxes of religion. Their revenge is both an act of horror and an apotheosis; it is a descent into barbarism and a leap into sanctity; it is an act of extremity that represents the contradictions inherent in any human action performed in the context of the world and what is beyond the world. It may be that in the story of revenge Elizabethan drama reached after its most religious statement; and that in Hamlet's revenge Shakespeare found means to picture the violence and pain that attend those moments when our secular lives are crossed by grace.

IV

But to think of the *Oresteia* is to realize how far Shakespeare's vision in *Hamlet* is from a statement of religious certainty. We know from Aeschylus that society, and divinity itself, may be transfigured; *Hamlet* is the story of one hesitant human being, and from his story we know only the dread of something after death, the fear that puzzles the will, and what Hamlet tells Horatio:

> For every man hath business and desire,
> Such as it is; and for my own poor part,
> Look you, I'll go pray.

Hamlet is a story of thoughts black and hands apt, at whose conclusion we tremble and look pale. There is, as Mr.

W. B. C. Watkins says, a "strong infusion of Christianity."
Yet this infusion of religious suggestion into a pre-Christian
story is "hard to judge precisely, since it conflicts with the
revenge morality." The play, Mr. Watkins says, has "a double
focus." Mr. Willard Farnham will not permit us to believe
that Shakespeare was concerned with this contradiction: "It
deserves all possible emphasis that Shakespeare does not make
Hamlet struggle with the inconsistency between a barbaric
tribal code and the Christian code of morals in the matter of
revenge, as a Christian Aeschylus might have made him
struggle. There is never a sign that Hamlet or anyone else
in the play recognizes this inconsistency, however much we
may recognize it and be tempted to read the tragedy accord-
ingly, or however much an Elizabethan auditor may have
recognized it in the light of the current condemnation of
revenge. Shakespeare is dramatically about other business."

But surely this inconsistency is in the play, whether we
recognize it or not; and it was Shakespeare's intention to
present still deeper inconsistencies. Shakespeare is dramatically about the business of picturing the contradictions
of any human act done between heaven and earth: religious
possibilities impinge upon Hamlet's natural situation, and
what are we to say about them? Nature is ambiguous and
heaven distant, and there is inconsistency in everything that
Hamlet does. It is after Hamlet has stabbed an old and innocent man that he says he is heaven's scourge and minister;
it is after bringing about the death of two fellow students
that he says a divinity shapes our ends; and it is after carnal,
bloody, and unnatural acts that Horatio would have flights
of angels sing him to his rest. There is in *Hamlet* a juxtaposition of religious possibility and events of savage brutality;
and this juxtaposition is a fact of Shakespeare's vision.

Dr. Johnson said that the particular excellence of *Hamlet*
is variety. It is a variety not only of what is done, but of what

is thought, the coinage of the brain. Laertes is quickly and completely committed to one course of action: he is wrong; his commitment is a repudiation of both the worlds, earth and heaven:

> To hell, allegiance! vows, to the blackest devil!
> Conscience and grace, to the profoundest pit!
> I dare damnation. To this point I stand,
> That both the worlds I give to negligence,
> Let come what comes; only I'll be reveng'd
> Most throughly for my father.

Laertes would cut Hamlet's throat "i' th' church." But Hamlet delays, and he has what Laertes lacks, the intellectual ability and moral willingness to encounter the contradictions that belong to playing the part of a son. Natural feeling is an honorable and valid persuasion toward sorrow, but our days of nature, seen against the hallowed time of grace, are frail and guilty; a human being is a god in apprehension and a quintessence of dust, brutal and holy, barbarous and sanctified, the instrument of heaven and when all's done the vice of the play and the fool of nature. In *Hamlet* Shakespeare's vision expresses itself through contradiction; the variety and incongruities of *Hamlet* are what make it seem more than a play; *Hamlet* is "the way things are." It is inconsistent that grace comes in violence, that revenge is a remedy, and that human life is attached both to the world and to what is beyond the world; the contradiction of action lies in its involvement both in time and in what is outside time. The fear and wonder of what it means to be touched by eternity is represented in Greek tragedy by the madness that overtakes those who speak to the gods face to face. In *Hamlet* it is figured in the address of the Ghost; in Hamlet's wild and whirling words; in his greatest soliloquy; and in the awe with which we witness his final words and watch his body borne to the stage.

V

After the storm in *King Lear*, the climate of the play seems changed; nature is cursed and ruined, but no longer fevered. Something has worked itself out, and there are no more appeals to the Goddess Nature and the natural powers, or to Apollo, Juno, and Jupiter. Lear and Cordelia will be God's spies; the name of God is introduced simply and easily, without our noticing. The natural setting is supplemented by suggestions of another setting, as if, in the progress of the play toward its own self-definition and identity, the context had altered and deepened to admit a further meaning.

This meaning is located in the figure of Cordelia; at her return she is stronger and lovelier than the folktale daughter who was too honest and too abrupt. France called her an unpriz'd precious maid, who was most rich being poor, and at her return she is surrounded by further paradoxical suggestions. Her love is not simply a natural bond; she describes it with words from the Christian story:

> O dear father,
> It is thy business that I go about.

She brings a remedy; Lear, who tore at his clothes when he confronted the thing itself, is dressed in "fresh garments," and he awakes at Cordelia's kiss of "restoration." The tears from her "heavenly eyes" are "holy water," and Lear asks: "Be your tears wet?" She seems to him to be a "soul in bliss." She asks Lear what he asked about himself: "Sir, do you know me?" And Lear answers: "You are a spirit, I know." In the corresponding scene of the subplot, Gloucester is restored from despair by his son Edgar; Gloucester falls from his imagined cliff, and when he wakes in the arms of his son, Edgar tells him:

> Think that the clearest gods, who make them honours
> Of men's impossibilities, have preserv'd thee.

Nothing almost sees miracles, Kent said earlier, but misery; and now Edgar tells Gloucester: "Thy life's a miracle." Gloucester will bear affliction and die when heaven pleases; Edgar has "sav'd him from despair." Lear and Gloucester are rescued by their children. But is Gloucester's life a "miracle"? And is Cordelia a "spirit"?

In the storm and on the verge of the cliff, Lear and Gloucester explore the furthest limits of what is natural in themselves and their children and their world. They discover unkindness everywhere; but it may be, in the failure of their natural philosophy, that they are ready to admit a new belief. Through their madness and despair they may have reached, in Mr. Eliot's phrase, a condition of complete simplicity, costing not less than everything. That condition, Montaigne wrote, "representeth man bare and naked, acknowledging his naturall weakenesse, apt to receive from above some strange power, disfurnished of all humane knowledge, and so much the more fitte to harbour divine understanding, disannuling his judgment, that so he may give more place unto faith." We have in *King Lear* a world reaching toward faith; and perhaps Lear and Gloucester, at the verge of natural belief, have won to a point at which, if it were permitted them, their belief might be completed.

But what are we to say of the "spirit" and the "miracle"? Cordelia "seems" to be a spirit, and it is suggested by her "seeming" that Lear's discovery of the thing itself may be supplemented by his discovery of Cordelia. A Gentleman gives the most puzzling description of her; she is, he says, a daughter

> Who redeems nature from the general curse
> Which twain have brought her to.

There is dissension over these lines. Mr. S. L. Bethell is reminded of Christ's redemption of cursed nature; and Mr.

Danby goes further by proposing that the twain who brought a curse to nature are not only Goneril and Regan but Adam and Eve. The play's latest editor, however, Mr. Kenneth Muir, finds this suggestion to be made "fancifully" — a word, such is the breath of editors, to fan a critic cold. Cordelia is not a symbol, Mr. Arthur Sewell says; she is "more humanly moving." Surely Mr. Sewell has the best of it; what is most affecting about Cordelia's return is that a daughter has come back to her father:

> Do not laugh at me;
> For (as I am a man) I think this lady
> To be my child Cordelia.

There are possibilities in Cordelia of a religious continuance; it is suggested that Cordelia in herself embodies an idea that might take the place of a belief in natural things, and like Helena in *All's Well* she joins heaven and earth in her own person. In the ruin of natural things and natural faith, Cordelia supplies a hint of what still remains; she is an evidence of things unseen; she implies that there is a further belief, and that if it were possible she would make our knowledge complete. But it is not possible; she is hanged; and the rest is silence. The most we can say is what Mr. Sewell says: "like the promise of rain in Mr. T. S. Eliot's *The Waste Land*, there are moments and images towards the end of *King Lear* which give promise of grace and benediction."

VI

We have spoken of likenesses between the stories of Hamlet and Orestes, and Lear and Oedipus. It is a notable fact that at their greatest moments the Greek and English dramatic visions expressed themselves through character and event that are so much alike; and it is a thought that gives an additional authority to the knowledge expressed by poetry and the theater. But how much more clear and certain is the Greek vision. When he wrote his memorial poem to Shakespeare, Ben Jonson summoned the names of Aeschylus, Euripides, and Sophocles. But Shakespeare is not, in Mr. Farnham's phrase, a Christian Aeschylus. And Sophocles' plays, Sir Maurice Bowra says, are "religious in a sense that Shakespeare's are not." They "display directly the relations between gods and men," and the field of their action is "the single reality to which both gods and men belong." Coleridge described the difference: there is in Sophocles "a completeness, a satisfying, an excellence, on which the mind can rest," but in Shakespeare there is "a blended multitude of materials, great and little, magnificent and mean."

In Sophocles' *Oedipus at Colonus*, Oedipus, like Lear, is moving toward death; and before he dies he is assaulted by the storms of the world:

> Think of some shore in the north the
> Concussive waves make stream
> This way and that in the gales of winter:
> It is like that with him:
> The wild wrack breaking over him
> From head to foot, and coming on forever.

There are discords in countries, division between brothers, and the bond cracked between father and child; the endless hours pile up a drift of pain:

> The immortal
> Gods alone have neither age nor death!
> All other things almighty Time disquiets.
> Earth wastes away; the body wastes away;
> Faith dies; distrust is born.

But how different are the deaths of Oedipus and Lear. Oedipus dies in thunder and lightning, but this is not Lear's storm, it is the final marvel of Oedipus' restoration. Colonus

will be his resting place, his holy and funereal ground: in
Oedipus the King, the fields of Thebes were barren and the
Theban women shrieked in childless pains; Colonus is shaded
with vines and olive trees and laurel, and gray-winged
nightingales sing in the grove. It is the place, in all the earth
and air, that is most secure and loveliest:

> No sun nor wind may enter there
> Nor the winter's rain;
> But through the haunted shadow goes
> Dionysus reveler,
> Immortal maenads in his train.

In the telling the beauty of this world becomes somehow the
beauty of the next; it is the first transformation, and the last
is Oedipus' death. Lear tears at his dress when he confronts
the thing itself, but when Oedipus undoes his "filthy garments" it is to prepare for his transfiguration. The thunder at
Colonus is the "God-thrown, the gigantic, holy sound." A
voice cries to Oedipus, and he walks into the light, dark with
excessive bright. It is Oedipus who leads the way and Theseus
who is blinded:

> We turned around — and nowhere saw that man,
> But only the king, his hands before his face,
> Shading his eyes as if from something awful,
> Fearful and unendurable to see.

Oedipus' death is "marvelous," and these things are "mysteries."

> But in what manner
> Oedipus perished, no one of mortal men
> Could tell but Theseus. It was not lightning,
> Bearing its fire from God, that took him off;
> No hurricane was blowing.
> But some attendant from the train of heaven
> Came for him; or else the underworld
> Opened in love the unlit door of earth.

Gloucester's life seems a miracle, Cordelia seems a spirit, and together Lear and Cordelia will take upon them "the mystery of things." But it is Oedipus whose death is in truth a miracle, and who indeed takes upon himself the mystery of things. Shakespeare's study of belief was written after sixteen centuries of Christianity; but it is the Greek play that ends with a religious statement, and with a vision of grace and benediction.

VII

The Greek theater had a special position in Athens, and a more than theatrical function; its festivals were religious festivals, with religious authority and privilege, and it included besides something of the philosophic discourse of the academy. Greek drama comprehended in itself the three great endeavors that in 1600 were undertaken separately: it united the knowledge of religion, natural philosophy, and art. There is no such conjunction in Elizabethan drama; by 1600 the English theater had won its independence from the church and stood free of its ecclesiastical origins, and apart from both the theater and the church was the new philosophy of natural science. Ways of knowing and replying to the world come together in Greek drama; but Shakespeare's tragedies are a way of knowing that is as distinct from the religious vision as it is from the scientific. The vision proposed in *Hamlet* and *King Lear* is artistic; it deals with the imagination, it offers its own way to be saved, and makes its own settlement between time and what is beyond time.

Warwick tells Henry IV that Prince Hal will in "the perfectness of time" cast off his followers. From their different points of view both Bacon and Spenser look toward this perfectness of time, the moment when our knowledge is completed; and Shakespeare's histories and comedies, and the last romances, record this same longing of the human spirit to end in a point of perfect order and perfect understanding. But what is made known in *Hamlet* and *King Lear* is the incompleteness of things in themselves and the uncertainty of what is beyond things. In the Red Cross Knight, Spenser wrote in his letter to Raleigh, "I expresse Holynes." In the figures of Hamlet and Cordelia we must say that Shakespeare expresses no more than the possibility of holiness. It may be that Hamlet's action and Lear's belief are Shakespeare's most religious statements: but the final assertion is never made; the last word is withheld; we have a sense, as we do with Chaucer's retraction at the end of the *Canterbury Tales*, of the incompleteness of art before a higher criterion.

Yet through the proposing and accepting of this incompleteness Shakespeare's tragic art arrives at its unique understanding of the two aspects of nature. The address that Shakespeare makes to the world is oblique and indirect; it announces not the perfect ensign of a single truth, but what is half thought and half expressed; it has a naturalness, and a loyalty to the variety of natural things. Hamlet is a son and Lear a father, and this, after all, is what is most stirring and important about them. Helena is a simple maid and therein wealthiest; the cunningest pattern of excelling nature is a woman, Desdemona; and the voice of the girl who redeems nature was ever soft, gentle, and low, an excellent thing in woman. When Jonson read Donne's *First Anniversary,* he remarked with asperity that if it had been about the Virgin Mary it had been something. Certainly in Hamlet and Cordelia, as in Elizabeth Drury, we have something else, more humanly moving. They are not figures in a religious equation; nor are they limited altogether to what they are in themselves; they represent a poetic and dramatic settlement between character and nature, an agreement that is never concluded, that is made and remade at every word they speak, and that is suggested in the equation that Jonson referred to when

he said: "I have considered, our whole life is like a Play."
What Shakespeare has to say about action and belief is
said in terms of the theater. The name of Shakespeare's play-
house suggests the close correspondence that can be drawn
between the stage and the great globe itself; and one reason
for the vitality of Elizabethan drama, and for its sense of
religious and philosophical as well as artistic importance, is
that this correspondence was drawn so often. There is not
merely a theatrical significance in the way in which character
declares itself on the stage; there is a moral and spiritual
weight attached to the manner in which character bears itself
in the world, and has its entrances and exits and plays its
many parts. Each thing that lives, Coleridge said, has its
moment of self-exposition. There is an assumption in Shakespeare's plays that the encounter between character and the
world is a dramatic encounter, and that in this confrontation
our greatest moments are those when we step forward to announce our actions or our beliefs, and hit upon the words and
gestures with which to say "I am that I am." When Shakespeare's characters announce that they are fools, or Hamlet
the Dane, their assertion has in it, certainly, the quality of
Homeric or Renaissance individualism — the flourish of declaring that "I am Odysseus," or that "I am Duchesse of
Malfy still." It is bravado, as Mr. Eliot says of Othello. Yet
it may be a kind of metaphysical bravado; it is the declaration
that character makes to the world to establish its identity and
take its place in the world. Hamlet's soliloquies are more
than a theatrical convention; they are made in reply to a profound necessity of human experience, the need for character
to stand alone and define itself. Though he assumes a posture
of doubt and uncertainty, he gives form to his uncertainty;
he creates himself; and though there is no one else on the
stage, we are his audience, and his words are made necessary
because of this sense of an audience. Sir Andrew Aguecheek

announces himself without being asked, but he does so nonetheless; as he says later about another matter, "I have no exquisite reason for't, but I have reason good enough." There is good enough theatrical reason for a character in a play to explain the way he acts and believes; though he gives a wrong explanation, as Iago does, still he tells us something of who he is. The persons of a play dramatize themselves; and in this there is a more than theatrical reason. A person in a play creates himself by his words; he becomes who he is by saying so. He demands that we give attention to his words and gestures, and if he is silent and unmoving, as Hamlet is when we first see him, he demands that we attend to his silence. The persons of a play are explaining themselves to their audience; they act and believe with the consciousness of being watched. In this lies a further correspondence between the stage and the world; for there is in our own lives a feeling that we play our part before a distant audience. There is a witness of what we say, like the mysterious presence in *The Waste Land* of "the third who walks always beside you."

It is this sense of the dramatic quality of natural life that suggests both the incompleteness of what we do and believe and the necessity of acting and believing. Through Hamlet's choice to act, even though his choice is no more than to walk in the hall, he makes his peace with the natural condition. Helena, in the world of comedy, resolves the two aspects of nature in her own person; and at the end of his life Hamlet accomplishes in his tragic world a similar resolution of time and eternity. What Shakespeare says in *Hamlet* about action seems to be something of this sort: there is an effort of the mind that looks toward perfect truth and holds back from accepting things in themselves, a desire to keep aloof from what is within change, and to come from the world's great snare uncaught; but there is another tendency of the mind through which character feels a deep engagement to the things of the world, and a necessity to share in their changes; and this necessity to take part in the world is the motive and cue for Hamlet's action. The necessity is stronger than his fear of the consequence; for it is the necessity to live, and in obedience to it Hamlet dies. To commit oneself to time and the world is an act of rashness, and Hamlet knows that this is so; to consent to the affections and allegiances of the world is to take the risk of playing one's own part in the world. Yet the need to share in the common natural history of life and death overcomes this consciousness that to act is to take a step into the dark and assume a position without grounds. And at the end there is more than this; at the mysterious moment when Hamlet accepts the challenge to the fencing match, a new possibility is made known. To share in the incompleteness of things is to find oneself made complete; by giving himself to mortality Hamlet becomes himself, and more than himself. His rashness is rewarded: his life reaches a point of perfect quiet and complete possibility, and in this moment of sudden comfort it is made known that to share knowingly in time is to arrive at an extremity of natural existence where the readiness is all, and where time and what is beyond time come together.

Bacon wished to explore things in themselves, and in *The Faerie Queene*, through the dark conceit of allegory, things are made to stand for the meaning of things. Shakespeare's vision is a way of knowing that is somewhere in between; at their greatest moments Shakespeare's tragic characters are touched by both things and meaning. By holding back from certainty, the tragic vision is increased by possibility, and persons and events are enhanced by seeming. Hamlet knows not "seems." Yet the stories of Hamlet and Cordelia are surrounded by seeming. Shakespeare's exploration of belief in *King Lear* is conducted in terms of paradox: duty in disguise, love in exile, reason in madness, sight in blindness, joy in sorrow, life in death, and heaven in a woman. Paradox is a manner of describing the natural condition that is central to Christian belief; but in *King Lear* it includes ironies that prevent the certainty of a religious vision, and that suggest a different way of describing what it means to believe. Nothing in *King Lear* is what it seems to be. At the division of the kingdom the children are not what they appear; Kent and Edgar assume disguises; and at the end the miracle that saves Gloucester from despair is not a miracle at all, but his child's pretense, an apparent miracle contrived by human affection. Lear dies in happiness, if Bradley is right, thinking that Cordelia lives: his last words are, "Look! her lips!" But it is not so; he is deceived; Cordelia is dead as earth. The play begins with the deception of the two old men, and at the end they are deceived once more. There is in *King Lear* a bitterly distressing discovery of the incompleteness of natural things in themselves. Something in the anguish of Hamlet's situation drives him to pretending, and the possibility is suggested in *King Lear* that in the face of such natural suffering there is nothing to believe in but pretense and show — a hundred knights or a gorgeous robe or an imagined miracle or a seeming spirit. The darkest possibility of *King Lear* is that only deception makes natural misfortune tolerable, that the unkindness of natural life is endured only through appearances, and that all that human love can offer, to show the heavens more just, is a trick. Yet there is comfort at the end of *King Lear*. What is mysterious about the concluding moments is that our minds are no longer pained by our knowledge that Lear is deceived, that Cordelia is not a spirit, and that there has been no miracle. In the eighteenth century *King Lear* was played with a happy ending. But the ending that we have is somehow beyond unhappiness. There is a necessity to believe, as there is for Hamlet to act; these are engagements to

incompleteness for which we can reason not the need. At the
beginning it is Lear's tragic mistake to attach his belief to
what his daughters seem to be; and the seeming of Edgar,
disguised as Poor Tom, is what turns Lear's belief to madness. But at the end it is in some fashion no longer a mistake
to believe in what appears to be; Cordelia's seeming is what
restores Lear's mind to sanity. It has been said that the tragic
protagonist advances through appearances to reality; and this
is true of Hamlet's and Lear's discovery of things as they are.
But it is true also that at the end of *King Lear* our thoughts
come to rest on appearances; it is enough that Cordelia seemed
a spirit, and that now she seems to live. We have reached a
verge of natural experience at which there are hints of the
vision that shapes the last romances: the rashness of action
and belief becomes a passage into seeming, and we are no
longer shaken by the difference between what is and what is
not; time is crossed by the continuance of time. Lear's discovery of the thing itself is supplemented by his discovery of
Cordelia; and when he tells her, "You are a spirit, I know,"
we have reached a moment when what is and what seems
come together in a new manner of knowing.

VIII

In Shakespeare's last plays, *Antony and Cleopatra* and the
four romances, we approach most nearly to meanings that
suggest allegory and a single reality. The tragic plot recurs
in a new proportion; there are dangers in the encounter between character and the world, but there is a greater certainty
about the remedies that restore the original goodness that
has been lost. The last plays, except for *Cymbeline*, are set in
Shakespeare's southern world; and the goodness of nature is
stated with confidence and wonder. Nature is a goddess, as
she is in the histories and comedies; she is "divine Nature,"
"noble Nature," "Great Nature," "wise Nature," the "good

goddess Nature," and "great creating Nature." Gonzalo's commonwealth is a dream of society in its original naturalness; and within the heart the natural principle addresses princes and lovers to instruct them in royalty. Marina and Perdita and Miranda, like Orlando in *As You Like It,* have a natural nobility; and they have more than this: nothing Perdita does but smacks of something greater than herself. The children of the Goddess Nature are innocent of their human parents' guilt; they repair the damage done by the older generation. Perdita is untouched by the "anger of the King" and the "trespass of the Queen." She redeems what Cordelia dies for, the anger of the King her father, and what Hamlet dies for, the trespass of the Queen.

Nature is the source of life and love, a seen and unseen lesson in goodness, and a creator of innocence and bounty — a perfect image, undoubted, unconfined, and unquestioned. Fact is replaced by the dream, and things are supplemented by powers beyond them; events are once more directed toward a happy ending. Pericles, like Lear, puts on fresh garments and is restored to his faithful daughter; Imogen is returned to her family and her husband; dear life redeems Hermione to Leontes; Prospero resumes his crown, his brother is forgiven, and Caliban will seek for grace. Even the death of Cleopatra is the moment of her wedding:

> Husband, I come.

In *Antony and Cleopatra* the visions of comedy and tragedy merge. And in *Pericles* a storm is a moment of both death and birth:

> Did you not name a tempest,
> A birth, and death?

The end of *Cymbeline* is a joining of heaven and earth:

> The fingers of the pow'rs above do tune
> The harmony of this peace.

At the end of *The Winter's Tale*, Leontes and Camillo look
as if "they had heard of a world ransom'd, or one destroyed."
Prospero and Miranda came ashore by Providence divine,
and by divine Providence Miranda and Ferdinand are in love.
Ariel's music is no mortal business, and Alonso says in awe:
"These are not natural events." Marriage is still a strange
eventful history, and now a continuance beyond nature is
drawing lovers to its bias:

> This is as strange a maze as e'er men trod,
> And there is in this business more than nature
> Was ever conduct of.

IX

The movement of the last plays is toward a moment outside time and change when a sense of persons and things is
transformed into a sense of wonder. Yet it is in the last plays
that persons and things in themselves are most wonderful.
Even in this final issuing of Shakespeare's imagination, its
deepest attachment is to the beauty of natural fact — the seasons, generations, and flowers; the lives of particular men and
women are a delight and wonder. There is a contrast frequently drawn in the last plays between natural fact and
human art; and it is nature that is the superior. Cleopatra
in her own person excels the fancies of art:

> O'erpicturing that Venus where we see
> The fancy outwork nature.

Antony in himself condemns the shadows of art:

> Nature wants stuff
> To vie strange forms with fancy; yet, t' imagine
> An Antony were nature's piece 'gainst fancy,
> Condemning shadows quite.

To praise art is to call it almost natural. Marina with her needle so composes

> Nature's own shape of bud, bird, branch, or berry,
> That even her art sisters the natural roses.

The cutter of Imogen's chimney-piece

> Was as another nature, dumb; outwent her,
> Motion and breath left out.

The statue of Hermione was made by that rare Italian master, Julio Romano, "who, had he himself eternity and could put breath into his work, would beguile Nature of her custom, so perfectly he is her ape." Nature and art are gentle rivals in the creation of the beautiful and wonderful, but art can never match the miracle of natural things.

Art breaks off; it cannot express the final touch; Julio Romano lacked eternity, and Imogen's chimney-cutter could not create motion and breath. The very source of art is nature:

> Yet nature is made better by no mean
> But nature makes that mean. So, over that art
> Which you say adds to nature, is an art
> That nature makes.

"The art itself," Polixenes says, "is nature." There is no design of art that is greater than that wonderful piece of work, a man or a woman. His enemies, Lear says, cannot touch him for coining: "I am the King himself," and "Nature's above art in that respect." Antony and Cleopatra are a Roman and a lass unparalleled; the return of Hermione is a human miracle of human love; and Miranda is

> No wonder, sir,
> But certainly a maid.

She is not a goddess, her lover says, but a greater wonder: "Sir, she is mortal." Art is what arranges the events of the romances; it is Prospero's "so potent art" that is in conduct of this business. Prospero presents a masque and draws his own play toward its happy ending, imposing his design upon persons and things; in what he does there is represented the power and beauty of art, and the effort by which the mind brings its own order and continuance to the world. Art is the miracle of the romances; Shakespeare's art makes itself known, declaring its own identity in the face of the world, and it is through the wonder of art that the romances approach meanings close to a single reality. But in the face of a human plot the actors of Prospero's pageant vanish to a *"strange, hollow, and confused noise."* We think sometimes of Prospero as the type of the artist; and we may imagine, if we wish, that there is an affinity between Prospero's art and Shakespeare's, suggesting the success with which Shakespeare imposed his own great vision upon the world. But what we remember about Prospero is only partly his success; it is partly the loneliness and melancholy that accompany this enterprise of the reason to connect things and their significance. It is Prospero who more than any other of Shakespeare's characters stands at one remove from the world, witnessing and guiding it, and at the end it is Prospero who will abjure his magic, break his staff, and deeper than did ever plummet sound will drown his book. In the mind of the artist is the consciousness that what he has chosen to do will never be completed; in the artist's inclosures of particularity there is a rashness that Jonson referred to when he spoke of Shakespeare's gentle expression and brave notions, and said that "Hee was (indeed) honest." And we think not only of Prospero, but of Hamlet, as close to Shakespeare himself; it is Hamlet who knows the theater, and what it means to stand aloof and play a part. It is Hamlet who holds back from conclusions, who is unresolved and uncommitted, and who has the ability that Keats said was Shakespeare's, Negative Capability, "when man is capable of being in uncertainties, mysteries, doubts." The artistic vision remains unfinished; and the rashness of Hamlet's residence among uncertainties suggests what it means not only to act, but to perform the continuous action of poetry, that is, after all, no more than seeming.

This sense of the incompleteness of art is represented in the last plays; and there is suggested at the same time the wonder of our belief in art. There is a necessity to perform the action of poetry, and there is a necessity to believe in its seeming. By our belief the dream is made fact. "I dreamt there was an Emperor Antony," Cleopatra says to Dolabella; his face, she dreamed, was as the heavens, his legs bestrid the ocean, and in his livery walked crowns and crownets:

> Think you there was or might be such a man
> As this I dreamt of?

Dolabella answers:

> Gentle madam, no.

But Dolabella is wrong. Antony lives in Cleopatra's dream; the truth and the dream are one. "The vision," as the Soothsayer says at the end of *Cymbeline*, "Is full accomplish'd." Things mingle with the mystery of things, action with acting, and belief with make-believe. We know from Robin Goodfellow that what passes on the stage is no more than a dream, and from Theseus that the best players are but shadows. The First Player weeps for Hecuba in a dream of passion, and Prospero's actors are spirits, and melt into thin air. The world of the theater is the fabric of a vision; like Tennyson's city of Camelot,

> there is nothing in it as it seems
> Saving the King; though some there be that hold
> The King a shadow, and the city real.

Camelot is never finished, and therefore always finished:

> They are building still, seeing the city is built
> To music, therefore never built at all,
> And therefore built for ever.

Shakespeare's last plays are built to music; they are indeed "a dream of learning." But the vision, because it is incomplete, completes itself; the seeming of the theater represents the seeming of the world. It is Shakespeare's last great character who says that we ourselves are the stuff that dreams are made on, and who turns aside to still his beating mind.

DATE DUE

DEC 20 '68			
FEB 27 '69			
GAYLORD			PRINTED IN U.S.A.